Prior to Consciousness

Also from the Acorn Press

I am that: talks with Sri Nisargadatta Maharaj. Compiled
and translated by Maurice Frydman; revised and edited by Sudhakar
S. Dikshit. 3rd ed., 9th printing, 1995. xxii, 550 pages, illus.
Paperback. **"A Modern Spiritual Classic."**
   Maharaj's unique teaching, in this compilation, has been hailed
as the direct path to the pathless goal of self-realization. The
central core of master's teaching: Until man can free himself from
false identifications, from pretensions and delusions of various
kinds, he cannot come face to face with the eternal verity that is
latent within his own self. "What the mind invents, the mind
destroys. But the real is not invented and cannot be destroyed ..."
says Maharaj.

*Prior to Consciousness: Talks with Sri Nisargadatta
Maharaj.* Edited by Jean Dunn. 157 pages, illus. Paperback.
(Selected talks, 1980-81.)

*Consciousness and the Absolute: the Final Talks of
Sri Nisargadatta Maharaj.* Edited by Jean Dunn. 118 pages,
illus. Paperback.

Pointers from Nisargadatta Maharaj. By Ramesh S.
Balsekar; edited by Sudhakar S. Dikshit. xvi, 223 pages.
Paperback. This publication is alive with the intensity and force
of Nisargadatta Maharaj's spiritual realization, and the fierceness
and dedication with which he relentlessly strove to accelerate
others' liberation.

*Explorations into the Eternal: Forays into the teachings
of Sri Nisargadatta Maharaj.* By Ramesh S. Balsekar. xiv,
261 pages. Paperback.

You may order directly from:

THE ACORN PRESS
P. O. Box 3279, Durham, NC 27715-3279. Tel.(919) 471-3842.
FAX (919) 477-2622

Prior to Consciousness

Talks with Sri Nisargadatta Maharaj

Edited by
Jean Dunn

The Acorn Press
Durham, North Carolina

First published 1985
2d edition, revised 1990
Reprinted 1997, 2004, 2007

ISBN: 0-89386-024-7
Library of Congress Catalog Card Number: 89-81145

Photographs by Gordon Paterson
Cover design by Joan Greenblatt
Cover art by Spar Street

Printed in the United States of America

The Infinite a sudden guest
Has been assumed to be,
But how can that stupendous come
Which never went away?
— Emily Dickinson

Bolts of Melody — New poems of Emily Dickinson
(New York: Harper and Row)

Preface

In one way the core of Sri Nisargadatta Maharaj's teaching is easy to grasp, and extremely difficult in another. It is easy if we are willing to be completely honest with ourselves, to look at the concepts of others with which we have built our own prisons. To investigate for one's self can be extremely difficult because we are very attached to our concepts — we don't want to give them up. But if the desire to KNOW is a burning desire, then we will set forth on our course. We can only know who or what we are by personal experience, not from books or others.

Maharaj urged us to find out what this "I" is. He was like a surgeon with a sharp scalpel, cutting away all inessential things. His questions often left one out in "left field," not knowing what to say. His answers were never what was expected. He would not allow any quoting of scriptures — only personal experience — and he could get quite angry about this. Once when someone quoted Dakshinamurti, a Hindu deity, Maharaj responded: "Hang Dakshinamurti! What about you? What is your experience?"

Most of us identify ourself with the body-mind and so he insisted that we find out what this body-mind is. Did it not come from the sperm of the father and the ovum of the mother? The body then is a product of the food consumed and is sustained by food, which is the essence of the five elements. Can we be this? Without consciousness the body is dead material. When consciousness leaves the body there is no individual, no world, and no God. Consciousness can only be conscious of itself when it has manifested in a physical form. Consciousness is latent in every grain of food, in all the five elements — it is universal, non-personal, all-pervading. Everything is consciousness, and that is what we are, presently. Consciousness acts through the forms according to the combination of the gunas, *satwa* (being-light-purity), *tamas* (inertia-passivity-darkness), *rajas* (activity-passion-energy), and to the conditioning received. What happens when one of these forms "dies?" The form again becomes part of the five elements and the consciousness merges with the universal consciousness. This is all a process happening, the play of consciousness.

Before this form came — what was I? That is what one truly is. That Absolute *Parabrahman* — these are only words which we have invented to name the Unmanifest, Unnameable. The eternal "I," absolutely unconditioned, timeless, spaceless, Being, not aware of being (because

vii

there is no other). I am as I Am, as I always was, as I ever will be, eternally.

Seekers from all over the world came to Sri Maharaj for his spiritual guidance. The contents of this book are transcribed from the tape recordings made during the question and answer periods of 1980 and 1981, until the death of Sri Maharaj from cancer of the throat on September 8, 1981, at the age of 84. Maharaj spoke only in Marathi and at each meeting there was a translator, not always the same one; we are very grateful to them. The most frequent ones were Sri S. K. Mullarpattan, Dr. D. Doongaji, Ramesh S. Balsekar, and S. V. Sapre (deceased), and the evening translator whom I remember only as Mohan. There were others at different times, but generally these were the day-to-day translators. We are also very grateful to Miss N. Vanaja who was so faithful in recording these talks.

During the last two years of his life Maharaj did not entertain any questions pertaining to this worldly life and its improvement. He taught only the highest truth, and due to the weakened condition of his body, on some days there was very little discussion. But even one sentence of his was like an *Upanishad*. He was very blunt and sharp in his answers and did not cater to anyone's ego — in fact, his stated purpose was to destroy this "psuedo-entity." To be in his presence was to feel the vibrant truth, impossible to describe. He was amazing to watch: that "personality" could be happy, angry, sad, gay, sarcastic, or gentle, and a variety of emotion played through that "bundle" like sunlight on water. There was never any attempt to change any of it . . . let it do its thing, it was not him. Suffering there was in abundance, due to the cancer, but in this human picture I have never seen anyone braver. Never did a whimper leave his lips. That body carried on when it seemed impossible that it could do so. One could only gaze at him in total love and awe. Although there was no doubt that the form of Sri Maharaj was suffering from cancer, he carried on just as usual with the daily routine of *bhajans* four times a day, question and answer periods twice daily, although as the body grew weaker these periods were often cut short. It was enough to be in his presence. It was only toward the end that he rarely spoke.

The repetitions in the text are necessary, as Maharaj hammered continuously at our concepts, each time bringing us back to the root when we tried to stray to the leaves and branches. When we tried to hang on to words, even words which he had used, he shot them right out from under us. As someone once said, "I am tremendously grateful to Maharaj. What is most different is that, regardless of anything, he answers what is most helpful and right, but people want to make the teachings into a system, which ultimately ruins them. But Maharaj doesn't worry. He just says on Wednesday that red is black, and on Friday that red is white, but the answer is correct at the time, because it changes the orientation of the questioner. It is tremendously valuable and unique." The reader should take only a few pages at a time and ponder and meditate over them.

If you read this book it is assumed that you have, as Maharaj said, "Done your homework." If you are ready to give up your identity with this pseudo-entity, read on and happy journey.

J.D.

April 4, 1980

Questioner: Would Maharaj talk about the grace of the guru?

Maharaj: It is the intensity of the faith you have in the guru's words that is most important; once that is there, the grace flows automatically. The faith in the guru is based on the consciousness within, faith in one's Self. The love for the beingness I am trying to direct to a higher level. What is lasting is this love for the Self, on which temples have been built. This Christ-consciousness is existing; is it faith in a man? As a man, Christ was crucified, but that universal consciousness which was his lives today.

Q: Is there a means of releasing or elevating this love?

M: That is a *vritti* (mental modification), that is part of the process. There are various actions, practices, etc. Even in daily life you have certain procedures; are they not the *puja* (worship) for this consciousness?

Q: Maharaj is talking about the kind of love that transcends consciousness itself?

M: The breeze that comes out of the universal consciousness is what keeps other kinds of love alive. Most people limit their love to an individual.

Q: How does one expand into universal love?

M: Understand the false as false, that's all you can do; you cannot turn one thing into another.

Q: Doesn't love lose its vitality when it loses its object?

M: You are asking from the body level, you are not going back to your state before the body came into existence. Before the word "love" came into existence, you are. Prior to this identification with the body, you must recede into That.

Since I have found my true permanent state I have no need for any of this, so I am just waiting for it to go. In that state of fullness there is no need at all. I have had this state of fullness after I met my guru; if I hadn't met my guru I would have lived and died as a man.

My association with my Guru was scarcely for two and a half years. He was staying some 200 kilometers away, he would come here once every four months, for fifteen days; this is the fruit of that. The words he gave me touched me very deeply. I abided in one thing only: the words of my Guru are the truth, and he said, "You are the *Parabrahman.*" No more doubts and no more questions on that. Once my Guru conveyed to me what he had to say I never bothered about other things — I hung on to the words of the Guru.

I know exactly what this present state of affairs is, how transient it is, and I also know that eternal state. I have no use for this ephemeral state. Now when you return to your country you will go with the qualification of a *jnani*. Tell me, what meaning do you attach to the word *jnani?*

Q: I think some of the Indians who have been here longer are more qualified, they might talk on it.

M: The present crop of Indians are following the Westerners who have developed so much on the material side. They are not after spirituality — they would like to follow Western scientific development, to imitate you. Because "I Am That"[2] is certified by Maurice Frydman they will read it; the books by Jean Dunn will have more significance also. I am not short of any knowledge relating to God or spirituality because I have fully known what this child-principle is. When you get to know that ignorant child-principle, beingness, you will not fall short of anything in your spiritual or worldly pursuits.

April 8, 1980

Questioner: Is the world as we see it, a thought? It is written in some places that when one sees the world one does not see the Self, and conversely, when one sees the Self, one does not see manifestation.

Maharaj: The world is nothing but the picture of your own "I" consciousness. As if you had received a phone call telling you that you are, and immediately the world appears. When you are in deep sleep and you feel that you are awake, the dream world appears simultaneously. With the "I Am," the world appears in the waking and dream states.

Q: Can one see the world without the presence of the ego?

M: When is there an ego? The ego is there when you have certain reactions. You take delivery of whatever is observed spontaneously. You cling to it, register it, then only is there an ego.

You see some building material lying on the road — you think that you are a carpenter and you start figuring how to use that material; the

---

[2] *I Am That: Talks with Sri Nisargadatta Maharaj,* translated from the Marathi taperecordings by Maurice Frydman, revised and edited by Sudhakar S. Dikshit, Bombay: Chetana; 1st American edition, Durham, North Carolina: The Acorn Press, 1982.

thought process has started, ego starts. If you are nobody, you will not bother about the building material — you will just observe it and go your way. Once it is out of sight it is out of mind; but when you receive that delivery, you cogitate over it, ego has started.

Q: So when it comes to the utility of what is seen, that's when the ego comes into being?

M: Yes. That is its nature.

Q: To get back to my other question, when the world is seen, the Self is not; when the Self is seen the world is not, is that so?

M: It is the other way. When you know that you are — the world is, if you are not — your world is not.

Q: Is "I" the Self? I am talking about the difference between the "I Am" and the thought "I am a man," which is the ego. In the "I Am" consciousness, does the world exist? Can you see it?

M: When you wake up you have only the sense of being, without words, this is the primary principle, the prerequisite; later on you know fully that you are and the world is, but that is an illusion, like the horns of a hare. The world is like the dream world, finally. Understand this point very thoroughly; you are dealing too much with the ego. Have you understood what was said about the ego?

Q: I think I have, if I ask another question maybe I can resolve it. Using the analogy of the snake and the rope (seeing a rope in a dimly lit place and mistaking it for a snake), if we use the world in that analogy where is the mistaken identity there?

M: The Self is the world. You are talking about removing the identity between the Self and the world, aren't you? First of all, dispose of the Self, understand what the Self is. Get to know the Self first, then get to know what the world is. The reason the world appeared is that you came to know that you are.

Q: How can one, in the waking state, lose the sensation of the world altogether and just be the Self?

M: You will have to consult the sun. Ask him, "How do you get rid of your light?" . . . light is the manifestation of the sun. Can you separate the light from the sun or the sun from the light? Because of the sun, the light is; because you are your world is.

Because the witnessing state happens, hence you are; because you are, witnessing is palpably felt; because the sun is, light is. If there is no witnessing, where is the witness? Dwell there.

Q: The being is the witness?

M: There are two witnessing stages; beingness witnesses all this manifestation. Witnessing of this beingness, consciousness, happens to that eternal principle, the Absolute.

April 14, 1980

Maharaj: So long as you are interested in this manifest world you have no time to get to the root. The root is this consciousness which appeared when you were a child. The root of whatever activities you are now doing is that moment when you were a child. In that child, the most important quality — the chemical, the consciousness — took the photograph. From that moment you started gathering knowledge and on that your present activities are happening.

People are so interested in my words that no one really tries to find out what that child consciousness is. Only when you get established in the consciousness can you know that child consciousness. That is the only way.

Questioner: Child consciousness implies a retrogression, as compared to the man consciousness. When in that state there is no consideration of child or man consciousness, there is just being — there is no further given direction.

M: There is no difference in the child consciousness and the man consciousness.

Q: If the space that fills the small pot is the same as the space that fills the big pot, how to recognize the small pot?

M: The seed of the universe is dimensionless but, because of the body, the consciousness appears and identifies with the body but actually everything is manifest, all-pervasive consciousness. That "I love" is manifest. For the whole universe there is no question of profit or loss, only when the identification with the body is present does the question arise.

When you take food, who is eating? The "I Amness." The food also contains the "I Amness," so when you consume it, you retain your "I Amness." Though the "I Amness" is in the food, nobody identifies with the food — they say, "this is my lunch; I am not this," but when it is consumed by them and becomes part of the body they say, "I am the body" — that mistake they make.

Q: I desire to be in the state of a jnani.

M: You have to know that knowledge "I Am." *Jnani* and knowledge are one.

Q: Just by being you have this knowledge?

M: You are already that, but you have to try to understand yourself.

Q: You understand that by the very essence of your being, so there is no knowledge involved.

M: At the moment you are identifying with the body, so you do not know that secret. You will come to know gradually, when you really become that.

Q: If there is only the sense of being in the "I Am," where do concepts come in?

M: Because of the vital breath, the mind flow is there. Mind means words, so thoughts are there — they are the concepts. Look at your root, the child consciousness, and finish it off.

Q: The difficulty lies in the fact that all consciousness is identical, so how to get to the root?

M: This consciousness is a tree, but there was a seed — go to the seed. The consciousness you have now is the same as the child consciousness; hold on to that, that is enough. So long as the consciousness is there everything is so important to you, but if that vanishes, then what is the worth of this whole world to you? Who is the knower of the seed? Give attention to how this "I Amness" has appeared — then you will know. Accept this identification only: that you are this manifest pure beingness, the very soul of the universe, of this life that you observe, and presently you are just wearing this bodily attire. Make a note of it; you have taken down so many things in life, just for fun, why don't you take this down also and see what happens? See what happens when you look at the moon and know that the moon is there provided you are there; because you are the moon is. This grand concept, this joy, you directly experience and enjoy.

Q: There must be some power which is responsible for this creation.

M: The power is the Self which each one has in his beingness — that power is time-bound. From the time that beingness comes it creates automatically until that beingness disappears. Earlier there was nothing — after there is nothing. It is only during the duration of the beingness that the world and creation is. This power is the faith in the primordial concept "I Am," and that is the concept which weaves the web of creation. The entire manifestation is an appearance in this concept.

April 15, 1980

Maharaj: When consciousness mixes with itself, that is *samadhi*. When one doesn't know anything — and doesn't even know that he doesn't know anything — that is *samadhi*.

Questioner: Will the body become rigid?

M: The body becomes still. Later on there is no realization of the body. When everything is accounted for, that is *sahaja samadhi*.

Q: The sensation is of glowing, effervescence, within and without; it provokes a little heat.

M: That is natural. When the five elements mix with each other, all kinds of things may take place. The five elements express themselves in different fashions through the body at that stage. This is not common to all, not necessarily uniform — each body will act and react in a different way. Therefore different Saints have different kinds of teachings. The common capital for all is the waking state, sleep state, and the consciousness "I Am."

Q: I did as Maharaj said. I examined the consciousness of a child, also I pondered about the seed and the tree, and I have resolved that equation.

M: What remains after those questions have been resolved? Can you do anything about it?

Q: No. The seed disappears into a seedling, the seedling into a tree and eventually the tree disappears. The seed of the child disappears into a teenager, etc.

M: It does not disappear, it is transformed. Now what remains is *Parabrahman.*

Q: There was the sensation of the son returning to the father.

M: Did that sensation happen inside or outside the source? The parents are only names given to the source which one always knows.

When something is understood, one does not really grasp it until a name is given and then one says that one has understood. The name is not the thing. Father, mother and child are three in name, but all three represent the same thing. What is is one only, *It* is, and the three are only names and numbers given to what is basically one thing. The union of *prakriti* and *purusha* is myself; *prakriti* and *purusha* are only names — they are not forms. This subject is meant only for those who are seriously interested.

The Jack fruit is a very big fruit with a thick skin and pointed stickers on the outside. Inside is the fruit, and within that is the seed. One uses the fruit, and the seed which is capable of producing more fruit is there. The human body is the same, what is outside is merely the shell; what one uses is the beingness inside. The seed can be used to reproduce, and the sweetness, the taste of "I Am," values itself and wants to continue at any cost.

Prior to taking this form you were formless; spontaneously the form came, and when the form came there was a natural longing to return to the formless state. When you want to return to the formless, desireless state, then only you come here, to seek what you are. The consciousness has to know the consciousness. When it realizes itself, then only do you return to normal.

Q: Has any one of those persons coming here become a jnani?

M: A number of those who have come here have acquired the knowledge, but only superficially. No one has really studied what the knowledge is; no one has really grasped the full meaning. What are they doing now? They are entangled in wanting, desiring, and this has made them forget the knowledge. Very few will get this knowledge correctly and absorb it deeply into their hearts. Once you have understood the origin of this movement, this activity, and the reason, the nature of this desire, then only can you return to what you are. Unless you are firm about it, you will not understand.

April 19, 1980

Maharaj: You have come here and you are sitting here, but this doesn't mean that you are expected to sit here for 24 hours continuously for days and days. You have come here for a short while, then you will go, again you will come. Like that, this body is a place for dwelling for a short while.

Having stabilized in the Absolute, the distinction is clearly made of beingness and prior to beingness.

Questioner: In the old days, it says in the Upanishads, *any disciple had to stick close to the Guru for one year without opening his mouth, and only then he could ask questions.*

M: When he sits in close proximity to a Guru the capacity of his beingness to receive this teaching becomes mature. His capacity to understand increases. It arises within him, it does not come from outside him.

You must come to a firm decision. You must forget the thought that you are a body and be only the knowledge "I Am," which has no form, no name. Just be. When you stabilize in that beingness it will give all the knowledge and all the secrets to you, and when the secrets are given to you, you transcend the beingness, and you, the Absolute, will know that you are also not the consciousness. Having gained all this knowledge, having understood what is what, a kind of quietude prevails, a tranquility. Beingness is transcended, but beingness is available.

Q: *What is that state?*

M: It is something like a deer taking rest in the shadow of a tree. The color of the shadow is neither light nor very dark, this is the borderland. Neither jet black nor very bright, halfway between them, that is that shadow. Deep blue, like clouds, that is that state. That is also the grace of the *Sat-Guru.* Everything is flowing out of that state, but this principle does not claim anything, is not involved in anything that is coming out of it, but this beingness is available. That deep, dark blue state, the grace of the *Sat-Guru.* This is the state of the *jnani,* this is a very, very, rare, natural *samadhi* state, the most natural state, the highest state.

You must have a firm conviction about this. Once the decision is taken, there is no moving away from it. The fruition of your spirituality is to fully understand your own true nature, to stabilize in your true identity. One must have patience, the capacity to wait and see.

The darkness that you see when you close your eyes, that is the shadow of the Guru's grace; don't forget it, always keep it in mind. Take rest in the shadow of the Guru's grace. Whenever you remember the words of the Guru, you are in the shade of the Guru's grace.

Ultimately, everything merges into the Self. You may come across great difficulties, but your courage and stability in the Self should be firm.

April 23, 1980

Maharaj: Be friendly with your undifferentiated state, your true Self. There was never any division, but you are under the delusion that you are not one with it.

I have understood my true nature: it is always alive, but not in the way everybody thinks. I don't wish to live in this life by the knowledge of the subjective world or the experiences of the subjective world. People are telling me that I must live; I don't want to live like that. I am alive because of my own nature, It is there, the existence is there, I am there only because of that existence. My true state, which is whole, un-differentiated, is beyond birth and death. I am never bound by my body and mind. I am limitless.

I, the Absolute, never had any experience that I was alive, and now I am experiencing that I am alive, and all this trouble I am experiencing through this I-am-alive-experience. This experience is limited to time and space; but when I understood the whole thing, I understood that I never had any experience that I was alive. That is a state beyond any ex-perience.

Why has this come? My Guru has explained correctly to me that the "I" consciousness appeared and these experiences started, so one can see the true nature of the "I" consciousness, go to the source, find out from where this "I" comes.

Questioner: What is the difference if I am sick and unconscious and Maharaj is sick and unconscious?
M: I know my true nature and I am That, while you are limited to your body and mind, therefore you might feel that you are sick now, so let the doctor come — he might do something. All those are notions you will have, but I don't have them. I am sleeping in my true nature, whereas you have taken a blanket and are sleeping.

Is it not true that when you are sick you are thinking only of your sickness? Why have you entered this field?

When I talk to you, don't try to understand from the body-mind identity. Your true state is always there; it has not gone anywhere. Although you did not know it was there, and now you know it is there, you have done nothing. It is always there.

On my true, whole, homogeneous state just a small ripple appeared, the news came, "I Am." That news made all the difference, and I started knowing this; but now I have known my true state, so I understand my true state first, and then I understand that this ripple is coming and go-ing on my true state. While, in your case, you take interest in the ripple and don't take interest in your true state.

Out of my existence as the Noumenon has come this state of the phe-nomenal. The homogeneous understands the play of the attributes, the projection of the mind, but the play, the projection of the mind, cannot understand the homogeneous. The moment it tries to understand It, it becomes one with It. Everybody is trying to understand the meaning of all this. You are not understanding because you have all the swaddling clothes of "I-am-this-or-that." Remove them.

The ultimate point of view is that there is nothing to understand, so when we try to understand, we are only indulging in acrobatics of the mind.

Whatever spiritual things you aspire to know are all happening in this objective world, in the illusion; all your activities, material and spiritual, are in this illusion. All this is happening in the objective world, all is dishonesty, there is no truth in this fraud.

Q: Last night, during meditation, there was a pure state of "I-I." I understood it to be recognition of the Self.

M: Is that the true meaning of your Self? Spit it out. Whatever you have understood, you are not. Why are you getting lost in concepts? You are not what you know, you are the knower.

April 30, 1980

Maharaj: This consciousness that "I Am" has created, and sustains, all the wonders in the world for which men take credit; on the other hand, this consciousness has no control over itself.

The principle out of which you have sprouted has tremendous powers. Lord Krishna has said, "You worship me, be devoted to me." This means what? The knowledge "I Am" which is indwelling in you — worship that only. You charge your beingness with those tremendous qualities of Lord Krishna; your beingness means Lord Krishna, be devoted to that.

In the initial stages, your devotion is of the surrendering type. You worship some principle and surrender to that principle. In the final stages you become the entire universe.

Your faith toward some principle will not remain the same; it will be continually changing.

All of you are like beggars; you have got a begging bowl and you want to collect God in that.

Take it that this "I Amness" of yours is the unadulterated form of Godlihood; the pure Iswara state is your beingness.

It is quite proper and praiseworthy that you are listening to the talks. Nevertheless, you are not getting rid of this attachment to the body-

mind. You are constantly surrounded by relations or intimacies connected with your body-mind. Have full faith in your beingness and
allow it to grow into the manifest *Iswara* principle. It is all powerful — meditate on that. It is very simple, yet at the same time, very profound. The consciousness is the seed of Godliness. If we give it its true
importance and pray to it, then it will flower into Godliness. If we don't
give it any importance, it will not flower into Godliness.

May 4, 1980

Maharaj: You understand yourself as body-mind; therefore my problem is — how to make you understand.

Lord Krishna said, "All are my expressions." The mountain is of
gold and a particle of that mountain is also gold. I am that mountain and
every particle is myself. The entire *beingness* manifest is myself, and each
being is a sample of myself. The knowledge "I Am" in each species is
myself. The very life force — luminous, bright, radiant, indwelling principle is myself.

If anybody understands me totally and fully and most appropriately,
that one gets the shelter in the shade of my benign being.

The state of a *jnani,* the highest state, has transcended the beingness,
but the beingness is still there, so together with the beingness is the Absolute — the deep blue, benign state, without eyes.

Knowledge takes rest in that deep blue, quiet, peaceful, benign
shade. When that shade is shifted aside, then he sees the various manifestations in the form of universes and worlds. But when the shade is
there, it is the deep, dark blue state, fully relaxed.

Questioner: Is Maharaj going to stop talking?

M: The talks will emanate provided someone worthy is there to put questions. I am nearing the end of my time. If any questions sprout, ask them.

Q: I want to stay here with Maharaj as long as possible.

M: Although you might go home, whatever has been planted, whatever
you have received, is going to change you. You are completely possessed.

Q: I feel that. I am grateful that at the tag-end of my life I was brought here.

M: Your coming here was also spontaneous. It is very rare that someone has the good fortune to come here; having come here, if the planting

is done, the sprouting will definitely take place. It may take time, but it will definitely take place.

Just as the beingness has appeared spontaneously, you don't know beforehand, now I am going to be — it has come about — so also the talks are coming spontaneously.

This touch of "I Amness" is in each being; this beingness has that touch of love for the Absolute and it is a representation of the Absolute. When you got yourself separated from the Absolute with this identity "I Am," you felt fragmented, isolated, and that is why your demands started. In the Absolute there are no needs. Only the Absolute prevails.

The truth is total Brahman only, nothing else but Brahman. In a total Brahman state the touch of beingness, "I Am," and with that, separation started, otherness has come. But this "I Amness" is not just a small principle, that itself is the *mula-maya,* the primary illusion. What I am expounding is not meant for the common people, because they have not reached the stature to understand what I am saying. Therefore I tell them to do *bhajans, japa,* meditation. After doing that, when the purifying takes place, they will be worthy enough to receive my talks.

Q: From the Unmanifest, the manifest is happening?

M: Who is asking this and why?

Q: I want to know.

M: Nothing prevails but you, everything is you. What answer can I give you?

If you want to remember this visit, if you have love for me, remember this "I Am" principle and without the command or direction of this principle, do nothing.

In the world today there are so many people and they are so busy with their affairs that they don't have time to eat — they *stand* and eat. These are characteristics of the *maya.* The great *maya* principle is making you do all her tricks, and you are also abiding in what she says, and finally, that light of yours, that beingness, gets extinguished. Then where are you going?

Q: I am going to search for another body!

M: This is all a concept. Before appearing in the world, do you remember your previous history, do you remember anything?

Q: No, but I have read . . .

M: I don't want to hear what others write, I want to know from the horse's mouth, from you. If you are not, can others be there? Is this not good enough for you?

Q: But I cannot think of a state when I had not been.

M: That was the non-attention *Parabrahman* state. That attention "I Am" was not there.

Q: Do we come from the Parabrahman *state and go back after beingness goes?*

M: Coming down into this world from the Absolute is something like the appearance of a dream. In a dream are you going somewhere? The primary ignorance is the understanding that you are the body. To know that you are the manifest is knowledge, and the knowledge merges into no-knowledge, *Parabrahman.*

Q: But I understand from the Gita . . .

M: Throw it away! Whatever you understand is not the truth and it is to be thrown overboard. You are trying to catch hold of something and cling to it. Accept, as it is, what I am telling you. Don't be carried away by concepts. Don't employ any words, and look at yourself as you are. Few people understand what I am driving at.

You are not paying proper attention, you are talking only after this beingness appeared. Before the beingness was there, look at that, be in that state. If you dare call me an atheist, remember that I do *bhajans* four times a day.

That *maya* is so powerful that it gets you completely wrapped up in it. *Maya* means "I Am," "I love to be." It has no identity except love. That knowledge of "I Am" is the greatest foe and the greatest friend. Although it might be your greatest enemy, if you propitiate it properly, it will turn around and lead you to the highest state.

May 8, 1980

Maharaj: After the information given to you by the mother, that you are a boy or a girl, all your further acquisitions are through hearsay. Your primary capital is knowingness, waking state and deep sleep.

Remember just this: a real disciple is ready to give up his body and the vital breath to attain this. Abide in the words of the Guru. Stabilize only in "I Amness."

The five elements and the three *gunas* make up your body and being-ness. When you abide in *Sat-Guru, Sat-Guru* indicates to you that you are the witness of your beingness also. Have faith in the *Sat-Guru,* you are

That. Such a *Sat-Guru* has remained untouched and without any stigma. Whatever is is there eternally, but we are overwhelmed by concepts. In the world of beingness the consciousness takes care of every worm, bird, human being, of all the species. That is the problem of the beingness. Every species knows the art of living.

Now it is said that I have a disease, therefore I have been taken to various eminent consultants and they have prescribed certain treatments. I have refused to take any treatment because the treatment is for the body and the guarantee of eternal life is not there. The promise was that I would be well for some time. I am not interested in such promises. I have stabilized in the Eternal and I am not fascinated by this type of life, this burden. I would like to get rid of that as early as possible, I am not interested.

Questioner: *You are the Protector.*

M: I'm not the Protector, the protection is automatically happening.

Q: *There are those well worth your protection; at least for them would you not listen to their advice, to give them satisfaction?*

M: That is not the way of getting satisfaction. To get satisfaction they should go inward. I am rather sorry that you are trying to do this spirituality in such a mundane manner. Suppose the so-called death happens to me, actually what is happening? There is the setting of the five elements, but I shall prevail always. I have stabilized prior to this beingness and the world. Whatever happens to the world, nothing happens to me.

The mind which was accepting that I was born is dead now. I cannot be measured by birth or mind.

There are so many so-called *jnanis,* but they are thirsty for worldly knowledge. Do you understand what I am driving at? You have craving for worldly knowledge.

You have the consciousness and you are trying to understand everything in this life. Can you control the consciousness? Can you keep it with you always? No, it can go at any time, and you have no authority that you can say this is my consciousness and I will hold on to it for such and such a time.

You are very fond of your dwelling-place in this world, this body. You would not like to go to a state which is beyond this, prior to this. You are enamoured of this beingness state.

May 11, 1980

Maharaj: In the body the consciousness does the witnessing; the behavior is done by the three *gunas*. Consciousness is all-pervading, spacelike, without form.

If one has an illness or a pain, is there a form to that? It is only a movement in consciousness. The knower of consciousness cannot feel the pain, and it is only because consciousness has identified itself with the body that the body feels pain. When consciousness is not there, even if the body is cut, there is no pain. It is not the body which feels pain. When there is a disturbance in the balance of the five elements, illness comes and the illness or pain is felt in the consciousness.

Just as in the winter the heat gets less and less, as this identification with the body gets less and less the pain that is felt gets less and less, to a degree that, with complete disidentification with the body, one can put his hand in the fire and not feel the pain. The effect of the fire will be there, but the pain will not be felt.

Now, say that I am feeling a pain at a particular moment, and something happens and my mind gets diverted. With this diversion of the new happening I won't feel the pain which I was feeling the previous moment. Many times I feel an itch all over the body and I scratch, but when sitting in public I don't feel like scratching, so I just tolerate it; in that tolerance it disappears. Otherwise, sometimes if we start scratching, even if the skin is scratched off and bleeding starts, still the itch will not stop. We have a saying in Marathi, "Don't provoke itching by scratching." Most pain and suffering is like this, if you pay attention, it is provoked and you have to pamper it. Don't pay attention, ignore the symptoms and they are lost. You must have the capacity to tolerate pain.

The consciousness in the body cannot have any blemish at all — that is the quality. But when you identify with the body, then, conceptually you might pollute it, but by nature it is very pure. Vital breath is very pure, and this beingness is purer than that. I am talking about *Atman,* the Self. This knowledge is likely to create a great sense of frustration in one who doesn't have the right perspective. The intention is to see the state of things in their correct perspective. Having seen it, live your life in the world to the best of your ability.

Immortality is beyond time and space; in that timeless, spaceless existence there is no entry for the five elements, for light or darkness, for the sun or the moon. Timeless, spaceless existence doesn't know that it is. That is reality, That is the truth.

In any amount of meditation, etc., you do not remain in your real state; it is only by firm conviction that you are the highest that you stabilize in the Ultimate.

Normally a common spiritual seeker will not understand what I am driving at because he is seeking something which he can enjoy. What is your ambition in being a spiritual seeker? You are looking for advantage in the world, to take care of your daily life — that is the maximum you expect out of spirituality. The so-called sages, who are following a spiritual pursuit, focus their ambition on seeing that their daily life goes on comfortably. Why in hell did I happen to be? Nobody enquires about that.

Only that person will visit this place whose virtue and sin have come to an end. So long as there is that stigma of the memory that you are a body-mind you will not understand.

The sum total of all this talk is known as *Sat-Guru-Parabrahman.* In that state there are no requirements. My state is that which never felt the creation and dissolution of the universe. I have not expounded this part. I remain untouched through the creation and dissolution of the universe.

June 27, 1980

Maharaj: The waking and sleep states and the "I Am" consciousness — these three are not your attributes but the attributes of that chemical. To what does the word "birth" apply? Is it not the birth of that which is in the body which makes it conscious? The chemical denotes the love the Self has for Itself and of which it wants to continue.

All experiences will be a means of suffering if one hasn't realized what they are. All experiences are due to memories and are merely movements in consciousness and therefore they cannot last. Happiness and unhappiness come and go. If you have a correct perspective, the world is still going on with a sense of quietude.

Nature has the institution of death. If death did not exist, there would be an unbearable accumulation of memories. People come and go, the memories are wiped out, therefore there is a sense of balance.

Questioner: But what is known to be temporary seems as if it were going to last forever when it is enjoyed. What is to be done?

M: Whatever you do will end in a calamity but you will not stop doing it because this is the nature of the body consciousness.

Death is considered to be a traumatic experience, but understand what happens. That which has been born, the knowledge "I Am," will end. That knowledge which was limited by this body will then become unlimited, so what is to be feared?

Q: My fear is not being able to love or be loved.

M: Please understand, feeling love for others, consciously and deliberately, cannot be done. That feeling of love must be understood and then love will unfold itself. Love for the Self, this consciousness, "I Am," those who have understood this as the true love, have themselves become love. All has merged in them.

This chemical which makes the body function is the smallest of the small, and the biggest of the big. It contains the entire universe, it is itself love and God. That chemical, the consciousness, provides the light which enables the world to get on. That love is not individual love; the indwelling principle in all beings is that love, the life force. Begin with this emotional love and dwell in your beingness. Whatever happens, happens in that which has been objectified in time and space; from complete absence has come plenty. The body is born, takes its space, and then it goes, but the Absolute is not affected. That eternal state prevails in spite of all happenings. Whatever tangible and visible world there is merges into nothingness. However that nothingness is also a state — so that nothingness also goes into the Absolute state.

Q: How did I happen to identify myself with the body?

M: What is this "I" to whom you are referring who has become entangled in the body and wants to know the answer?

Q: I don't know. Why is it that I cannot know who I am?

M: I can only know something different from me. How can something know itself when there is nothing with which to compare? It is alone, without identity, without attributes. We can only talk about it at the phenomenal stage.

I have got this illness. What is the illness and on what has it come about? The illness is not separate from what exists as the body, breath, and the knowledge "I Am." This is one bundle which has been created, whatever happens is contained in that bundle. I have been separate from it before conception, and I continue to be separate from what has been created. It has happened, it will continue for a while, then it will go away. Time has brought this about and time will end it.   Is not what was conceived and born the same now? That "I" has not changed from the conception till the present moment. It has come for a particular length of time.

What was conceived has grown physically, and some of the expressions of this knowledge "I Am" have achieved tremendous things. Some have became *avatars,* some have achieved success in various fields. At the end of the time span the magnificent personalities, and whatever they have achieved — both have disappeared. It may have been for many years; this "I Amness" may have remained existent for hundreds of years in particular cases; still, however long the time, there is an end to it.

Some of these *avatars* and *jnanis* have understood what the "I Amness" is, that it needs a body before it can manifest itself, and the body can only come out of sexual intercourse. Having understood it, instead of remaining in that knowledge apart from manifestation, and merely observing manifestation, they started giving advice to that which is only conceptual; all manifestation is conceptual. They said, "Let there not be sexual relations." Many of these *avatars* and *jnanis* have given this advice. Has it happened? Has the rain stopped? Has the production of population stopped? No. Nature will take its course. It is only to be understood, nothing is to be done.

Remember only one thing: that it is this "I Amness" which has remained unchanged at all times, and which pervades the entire universe. It is the highest God as far as this manifestation is concerned.

Ultimately even this is temporary, and what I am is prior to the senses, spaceless, timeless, without attributes, but in the manifestation this "I Amness" is the highest God and you must be one with that.

Q: When the body dies is there a question of rebirth if I still identity with the body?

M: So long as you identify with the body, whatever is written in the scriptures you must follow. When you lose your identity with the body, then you can do whatever you like.

June 29, 1980

Maharaj: Whatever concept you have about yourself cannot be true. The "I Amness" is the prime concept, and it has to be satisfied by letting it do its normal work in the world. The important thing is the realization of the fact that it is a concept.

Questioner: In the world this concept is always trying to be at the top. Even to the children we say, "You must be first in the examination." Is it wrong to push your personality and individuality on others?

M: What is wrong is that you consider yourself to be limited to this body and shape. What knowledge I try to give is given to the knowledge "I Am" in each of you, which is the same. If you try to get that knowledge as an individual you will never get it.

Q: If "I Am" is a concept and it disappears, how is one to know that that concept has disappeared?

M: That "I Am" is a concept is to be understood while the concept is there. Once it merges in the original state, who (or what) is there who wants to know? The illusory entity has disappeared.

Q: I am convinced that this "I Am" is a concept and it will end, but why should I take it that it is a false concept?

M: How and when did this very thought come? Did this thought not come merely as a movement in that concept itself? If the consciousness were not there, the thought would not be there.

Consciousness is a temporary condition which has come upon the total, timeless, spaceless, changeless state. It is a happening which has come and which will disappear.

This psychosomatic bundle which is born will suffer or enjoy during its alloted span; so long as I know that I am not the one who experiences, but I am the knower, how am I concerned?

It is perfectly clear. I merely watch the body, mind, and consciousness laugh or suffer. In suffering it may cry out, all right, cry out. If it is enjoying, it may laugh. I know it is a temporary thing, if it wants to go, let it go. While I am talking to you, imparting knowledge, at the same time I am feeling unbearable pain, if it becomes a little more unbearable I may whimper. It can do what it likes, I am not concerned. So long as you have not known what this consciousness is, you will fear death; but when you really understand what this consciousness is, then the fear leaves, the idea of dying also will go.

This consciousness is time-bound, but the knower of the consciousness is eternal, the Absolute.

July 1, 1980

Maharaj: Once the body is gone, that knowledge which experienced itself as Christ, Krishna, Buddha, etc., has subsided, has become one with the total. If you abuse them by word, they do not come and ask why you are abusing them, because that knowledge which experienced itself as one of these has subsided into the totality. Similarly now, you might be a very great person but when you go to sleep you forget yourself as a separate entity.

Don't say that you are an individual; just stay in the beingness. The whole problem is the sense of being a separate entity — once that subsides, that is true bliss. With the arising of the "I Am" the whole of manifestation takes place; in any activity that which witnesses is the "I Am," that which is doing all this is *maya*, the tendencies, attributes. This is what I am trying to tell you, but you want something else, something that is in the manifestation — you want knowledge.

That knowledge "I Am" is new, it is not the Real; the Real I am not telling you, words negate That. Whatever I am telling you is not the truth, because it has come out of this "I Am." The truth is beyond expression.

You are going all over, amassing knowledge for an individual. This amassing of knowledge is not going to help you, because it is in a dream.

Questioner: *How does Maharaj feel about all the people coming here?*

M: I don't care. You come and listen to me and go. If you want it, take it. If not, go away. The space in this room is neither for, nor against, nor in love with, the space in that room; it is one.

Like a river flowing, if you want to utilize it, you take the water and drink it, assimilate it; otherwise, let it flow past. I am not charging you, just like the river is not charging for the water. You are spending a lot of money every day; come on, you put your money away and take my water.

While talking about it I take you to the source of the spring; there water is coming out in a trickle. This water afterwards becomes a river, an estuary, becomes the sea. I am taking you again and again to the source. Once you go to the source you will come to know there is no water actually, water is the news of "I Am."

There is only one principle, the principle "I Am." Because you are, everything is. Hold it close. You have heard, now live accordingly.

Q: *My work as a doctor keeps me constantly busy, how can I do as Maharaj says?*

M: You are engaging in worldly activity everyday, but before you go to sleep at night forget all that, and think of what I have told you. Take one sentence of what I have told you and stay with it; that will lead you to your source. *[Maharaj tells a story]:* A person meets a man and the man gives him something to drink, then he tells him, "I have put poison in that drink, and in six months you will die." That person becomes very frightened and believes that he will die in six months. Later he meets a friend, and tells him what has happened and that he will die in six months. His friend tells him not to worry, and says, "Here, drink this, and if you drink it there will be no death for you." So the fellow is happy and drinks it.

With the first concept he is full of fright, and convinced that he is going to die; later on, the friend gives him another concept which negates the first concept. This is one of the attributes of the vital air, getting concepts, ideas, creations, again and again. It is only when you search for your Self that you become aware of this.

The very source of all happiness is your beingness, be there. If you get involved with the flow of *maya* there will be misery. You try to derive pleasure from the activities of *maya,* this is the product of beingness. Be still in your beingness.

What I have told you, remember it, chew it, recollect it. It will lead you to the stillness. Establish in that knowledge.

Q: What will happen?

M: It will be clear to you, just as clear as seeing the five fingers on your hand. You observe, this body is made of the five elements, and because the five elemental body is there, your beingness, the consciousness has appeared.

Your beingness is there because of this food body and the vital breath, and you will be able to watch all these elements — the body, your vital force and your beingness; but you must be established in that knowledge. In short, you liquidate that yardstick of body-mind as your identity. When this is done, you are *Iswara,* you are Brahman.

Q: Then how do I elevate it to a higher level?

M: Leave it alone! There is no question of elevating to a higher level. Here it is only a question of understanding.

Iswara is the manifestation of the five elements and the universe, the "I Amness." To the Absolute, the witnessing of that "I Amness" occurs. This is the Absolute standpoint, *siddha.* This understanding should not be claimed by you, who are a *sadhaka. Sadhaka* means the process of getting established in the *Iswara* principle, the consciousness.

Q: Last night there was an experience of very great vibration in the body. In fact there was no body, just vibration, no form, and very intense.

M: Whatever that vibration, that is the product of the five elements.

Q: It is not a taste of "I Amness"?

M: If you want to express it that way, you may. These are the five elements, three *gunas, prakriti* and *purusha,* ten elements. These are the expressions of your beingness.

Q: So when Maharaj says to stay firm in the consciousness of not being the body-mind, how does that relate to these ten elements?

M: That talk — to transcend the body-mind and establish in your beingness, is for the kindergarten spiritual seeker, the lowest level. But now I am talking to a *sadhaka* who is getting established in beingness; that first lesson is over now.

Q: Oh!

M: Your world, your universe, is the expression of your beingness. The second step, the *sadhaka* gets established in beingness, *Iswara* principle, manifestation. A *sadhaka* is manifestation.

Now, after listening to all these talks, he will leave this place and tell people that he meets, "I have met a Maharaj who was talking, and he has added confusion worse compounded."

Q: Maharaj's teaching is very clear. The only thing is that it is happening so fast, and that it is clear, so fast.

M: This manifestation is Self-effulgent, Self-created, but you are still wanting to modify something, you are not through with this.

Q: That is what I am saying. The consciousness is aware of being everything, that it is Iswara, *then because of some firm-set habit of the body-mind state, all of a sudden, spontaneously, comes a desire to modify, or adjust everything, and, at that moment something else happens that says, "you can't adjust it, it is as it is." That is what has been happening.*

M: See that you are not involved in that.

Q: That is why it is so helpful for me to be here.

M: The Absolute is aloof. In the sleeping state the "I Amness" goes into oblivion, he forgets himself. "I Amness" is subjected to the waking and deep sleep states, but the Absolute is also that. You will not comprehend exactly what it means, but as you get established in beingness and transcend that, you will understand how you are beyond deep sleep and waking, because those are only the characteristics of the beingness.

Q: That Absolute, is He aware what is happening when that "I Amness" goes to sleep?

M: "I Amness" is a sort of tool, with "I Amness" only He observes. You entertain some concepts, when you listen to me. If you hear something that tallies with your concepts you are quite happy — you say it is knowledge — but I completely blast that. I want to blast all concepts and establish you in a no-concept state.

Your beingness is the subtlest, at the same time it has gross qualities latent in it. Take the seed of the banyan tree: it is very small, very subtle, but all the gross matter is already there, inside. Your beingness is the subtlest, and still it contains the entire universe. It is a continuous process; the seed contains everything, repeat, repeat, repeat. The so-called spiritual seeker wants Brahman, but how? As he orders, the Brahman should happen like that. According to your concepts, you want to re-create the Brahman.

Q: Which just brings you further from the truth.

M: Everything is the truth — the Absolute. Brahman is created out of your beingness. All this Brahman is illusion, ignorance. Your beingness is ignorance only, from the Absolute standpoint.

When you pursue this spiritual path of understanding the Self, all your desires just drop off — even the primary desire, to be. When you stay put in that beingness for some time, that desire also will drop off; you are in the Absolute.

Q: That is what was happening today, and there is a certain sadness, in realizing that, and yet, a great understanding of the Absolute.

M: It is only that consciousness constantly repeating, receding from the Absolute, there is no movement for you — It is minding the show.

When you are in consciousness, you understand the nature of consciousness. This consciousness is extinguishing, knowingness is disappearing, but nothing affects you, the Absolute — that is the moment of death, but what matters? The vital breath is leaving the body, the "I Amness" receding, but the "I Amness" is going to the Absolute. That is the greatest moment, the greatest moment of immortality. The "I Amness" was there, that movement was there, and I observe, it is extinguished. The ignorant one will get very frightened at the moment of death — he is struggling — but for the *jnani,* it is the happiest moment.

July 6, 1980

Maharaj: Whatever goes on in the world is based on the life force *(prana shakti),* but the *Atman,* the witnesser, is totally apart; no action can be attributed to the *Atman.*

So long as you have not understood *prana shakti,* the vital breath, whose language is the four types of speech which flow through the vital breath — so long as you do not recognize it, whatever the mind tells you you are bound to take as certain. Those concepts which the mind gives you will be final for you.

Questioner: *What are the four types of speech?*

M: They are, *para* (source-consciousness), then *pashyanti* (the emanation of thoughts), then *madhyama* (formulation of thoughts-words), and *vaikhari* (language explodes out). The ordinary ignorant person is not aware of *para* and *pashyanti,* which starts the whole process, they are too subtle; he starts working on *madhyama,* which is also identified with the mind, and comes out with words *(vaikhari).*

The mind throws out words and thoughts, and through these we have mistaken our identity as "me" or "mine," whereas whatever takes place is independent of the one who witnesses and is based entirely on the life force. This consciousness has mistakenly identified itself with the body, and with thoughts or words. It considers itself to be guilty of something, or that it has acquired merit by some action, whereas everything merely takes place through the action of the life force.

The one who understands this vital breath, the life force, is beyond all mental concepts. The one who has not understood it is a slave to his thoughts.

Q: *After prolonged use of the* mantra, *will it get dissolved?*

M: Both the *mantra* and the faith in the *mantra* will get dissolved. There is a purpose in the *mantra.* In India the *mantra* has great efficacy. By concentrating on the *mantra* the form behind the *mantra* will appear out of the ether, but all this is time bound. Man has evolved all kinds of things for his own preservation, the preservation of the consciousness.

I am not any longer concerned with, and no longer want, the continuation of either the body or the vital breath.

That bundle of three states and three attributes[3] has been born, and whatever happens, happens to that bundle, and I am not concerned with it. That is why I am totally fearless, without any reaction to a disease which would be traumatic to others.

Having known that I am not that which has been born, yet there is some little attachment to that with which I have been associated for a long time — it is a speck of attachment because of eighty-four years' association. Say I meet someone from my hometown whom I have known

---

[3] Waking, sleep and "I Am" consciousness — the 3 *gunas* — *sattwa, raja, tamas.*

for a long time, he comes and he goes away, so I bid him goodbye, and there is that little speck of attachment, because I have known him for a long time.

The consciousness which is born thinks that it is the body and works through the three *gunas,* but I have nothing to do with this, the whole thing is an illusion.

Q: Will there be no continuation of memories after death?

M: Only if there is sugar cane, or sugar, will there be sweetness. If the body is not there, how can there be memories, the beingness itself is gone.

Q: How does one know what remains?

M: There are twenty people in this room, all twenty people leave, then what remains is there, but someone who has left cannot understand what it is. So in that *Parabrahman* which is without attributes, without identity, unconditioned, who is there to ask?

This is to be understood, but not by someone: the experience and the experiencer must be one, you must become the experience. What is this *Parabrahman* like? The answer is, what is Bombay? Don't give me the geography or the atmosphere of Bombay, give me a handful of Bombay. What is Bombay? It is impossible to say, so also with *Parabrahman.* There is no giving or taking of *Parabrahman,* you can only be That.

Q: We want the state which Maharaj enjoys.

M: The eternal Truth is there, but for witnessing it is of no use. You give up this study in the name of religion or spirituality, or whatever you are trying to study. Do only one thing, that "I Amness" or consciousness is the Godliest principle; it is there only so long as the vital breath is there — it is presently your nature. You worship that only. That "I Amness' is something like the sweetness of the sugar cane, abide in the sweetness of your beingness, then only you will reach and abide in eternal peace.

Q: I feel the life force energy polarized and intensified in my body in the presence of Maharaj.

M: In practicing meditation the life force gets purified, and when it is purified the light of the Self shines forth, but the working principle is the life force. When this purified life force and the light of the *Atman* (Self) merge, then the concept, the mind, the imagination, everything is taken away. The life force is the acting principle and that which gives sentience to the person is the consciousness.

Q: This is what the tradition of shiva *and* shakti *signifies?*

M: *Shiva* means the consciousness and *shakti* is the life force. People go by various names which have been given, and forget the basic principle.

Merely sit in contemplation and let the consciousness unfold itself. What have you understood?

Q: *This consciousness starts to get a greater sense of itself, and the* prana *and the body's energy becomes intensified and polarized, it seems to be part of the purification.*

M: When this consciousness and the *prana shakti* (life force) merge, they tend to go and become steady in the *Brahma-randra,* and then all thoughts cease. This is the start of *samadhi.* Then one comes back again and the life force starts its normal activities.

July 9, 1980

Maharaj: Understand that it is not the individual which has consciousness, it is the consciousness which assumes innumerable forms. That something which is born or which will die is purely imaginary. It is the child of a barren woman.

In the absence of this basic concept "I Am" there is no thought, there is no consciousness.

Questioner: *Maharaj has said that if you stay in the consciousness, the beingness, it will automatically happen, that you will transcend the consciousness. Is this true, there is nothing more to be done?*

M: Suppose I am sitting here and you come, I come to know that you are, the witnessing happens automatically. Has anything been done? No. It is like that. It is simple. You should understand. Just like a raw mango becomes a ripe mango, it happens. Many people get satisfied in the consciousness state.

Q: *I am not going to be satisfied until I am in Maharaj's state.*

M: Whatever you consider yourself to be at the moment, when you get rid of that, whatever your true nature, it is spontaneous. Abide in the words of the Guru.

Q: *When you read Maharaj's teachings you want very much to be in his company. There is something very enlivening about that. Is it important or essential?*

M: It is very advantageous to get rid of all your doubts. That's why the questions and answers are required. This is the place where you get rid of all concepts. The trees which are near the sandalwood tree also have the same smell, because of proximity.

What is the Self? If you want to expand, the entire world is the manifestation. At the same time it is very tiny — the seed beingness — like an atom, a pinprick of "I Amness."

That is the very source of love. Such a potential is there, having provided that love to the entire world, it remains in that seed "I Am," the leftover is that "I Am." That pinprick or touch of "I Amness" is the quintessence of all essence.

One must have firm abidance or faith in the words of the Guru. Here I do not repeat or imitate what other sages do. I am not championing any religion. I have no pose or stance for anything, not even that I am a man or a woman. The moment you accept any pose or stance you have to take care of that by following certain disciplines relating to that pose. I abide in the Self only.

I do not believe that anybody did exist prior to me. When my beingness appeared, then everything appeared. Prior to my beingness, nothing was. Originally I am without any stigma, uncovered by anything.

The *Paramatman* is the core Self, the highest Self. Its identity is without any stigma, it is subtler than space.

Why are you dying? Understand the first moment, when you understood that you are. Due to what? How?

Once you understand this, you are the highest of the Gods — the point at which everything rises; the source and the end is the same point. Once you understand that point, you are released from that point. Nobody tries to understand this happening of the "I Amness." I, the Absolute am not this "I Amness."

In meditation your beingness should merge in itself, a non-dual state. Remain still. Do not struggle to come out of the mud of your concepts, you will only go deeper. Remain still.

July 15, 1980

Maharaj: What is the effect of what I have spoken on you?

Questioner: Whatever Maharaj has spoken is the truth, but I also request him to show me a way. Maharaj says that sadhana *is not the way, but the determination that I am the consciousness is a very difficult thing. I am practicing.*

M: Who is practicing? It has no form, it is dwelling in this body. How long will it continue and what is the gain? Abide in the Self only. Until then it will continue the *sadhana;* once it is established in the Self, the objective, the person who is practicing, and the process of practicing is gone. A *sankalpa* indicates a need, an objective.

Q: *What is a* sankalpa?

M: You want a medical degree, that is the *sankalpa. Sadhana* is the study, practice, homework. You wanted to meet me today, that is a *sankalpa.* You walked here and climbed the stairs, that is the *sadhana.* That *sankalpa* has no form, the one who makes the *sankalpa* also has no form. So long as you are identifying with the form the practice will go on. Once you reach the objective, which is that you are not the body-mind, then there is no practice.

You have great faith in the *Bhagavad Gita:* is this correct?

Q: *Yes.*

M: *Gita* is a song sung by Lord Krishna. He sang the song just as I am singing this talk to you now; this is *Rg Gita.* You have read the *Bhagavad Gita,* recited it, remembered it; but what is important? You must get to know that Krishna who sang that *Gita.* You must get his knowledge, what he is.

Is it not an incarnation? In short, from nothingness the form is taken; the nothingness descends into form, that is *Avatar.* Normally we say from nothingness a person is there, but for these great personalities, great sages, you will say *Avatar.* Are you trying to understand that Krishna? No, you are creating certain concepts and trying to understand him. That is not correct. From nothingness he was — how did it happen? This incarnation you must understand, the descending into *Avatar,* or form; what is this? Prior to incarnation that personality had no knowledge about himself, after descending into this incarnation he started knowing himself. What are your comments?

Q: *Before* Avatar *he had no knowledge of himself?*

M: Before descending into this *Avatar* this knowledge quality is not there.

Q: *But* Parabrahman . . .

M: These are all conceptual titles and names; they are shackles on you. In your core Self there is no imposition of any title or name, externally you have accepted them.

Any embodied person with the knowledge "I Am" carries on his activities in the world with the name only. That inner core, the "I Am" has no shackles. Once it is understood that I am that "I Am" only, and not this shackled form, then no liberation is called for; that itself is liberation.

You know the historical facts about Sri Krishna by heart, but you must know what this incarnation is. Names are the handcuffs, the bondage. Every person is shackled because of his identification with the body. Without that name and form, please proceed to talk and question.

Q: The only words I have are very much words with name and form. They are words of gratitude. Gratitude for what Maharaj has blessed me with since I have been here. To even see a sage in one's lifetime would be an incomparable grace, and to have had so much grace from him in the form of his instructions just overwhelms me, and there is absolutely no way I can ever thank him.

M: What do you mean by grace? Grace means that you have come to me. *I* and that *you* are only one. That you understand that we are one is grace.

Q: At times like these that is the hardest thing to understand.

M: Grace means totality, wholeness, there is no fragmentation.

Q: [another] Why I am ostracized? Why can't I see the truth?

M: You are ostracized because you are identifying with the body-mind and the memory that you are a body. Give up that identity, and that memory, and then whatever you see will be the truth.

This is a very rare, a very precious opportunity, wherein you get this conflux of three entities: body, vital force and the touch of "I Amness," and with this alone you can reach right up to the Absolute — you can abide in the Absolute.

In the name of spirituality people carry out various types of acting, like *japa,* penances, etc. Once you accept that actors pose, you undergo the disciplines and therefore all the sufferings are related to that. This is not going to lead you to the Ultimate, the Absolute.

For you, the first step is worship that vital breath; here you must focus your attention on that vital breath pulsation — and together with that, carry out the name-*japa.* When you do that, the vital breath will be purified, and in the process of purification this beingness will open up. Just reciting the name of God is concentrating the vital breath. The meaning of the *mantra* is that you are not the name or form.

All the 24 hours this vital breath, or vital force, through various perceptions, is recording the pictures of all your experiences and memorizing whatever is relevant. Can you do that with your intellect?

Q: [newcomer] I saw the article in the Mountain Path[4] *about Maharaj and I have come to ask his blessings.*

M: Your spiritual acquisitions, everything is very good, but when you finally realize yourself you will come to the conclusion that all is useless, redundant, superfluous.

Q: That is why I am asking for the blessing of Maharaj — to have that experience.

M: In that highest state there is no experience. Experience, experiencing, experiencer — everything is only one.

Q: Can Maharaj give a push to reach that state?

M: Somebody has already given a push to you and that is why you have come here. From the front you are pushed backward. Recede into the source. *[To another]* Has your talking machine gone out of order?

Q: Before I acquired this body, did I know everything?

M: You were perfect, total.

Q: Just because I am encased in this body I am suffering.

M: How did you reach your parents? Deliberate on that.

Q: I had the desire?

M: For the time being let us assume that you had the desire, but just tell me, how did you reach those parents?

Q: I do not know.

M: Whatever you do *not* know is perfect. Whatever you *know* is imperfect, fraudulent.

Q: Just because I am encased in the body I am in agony to be perfect, which I am not.

M: Why do you worry about this encasement in a body?

Q: Who is worrying? That cannot be me.

M: The worrier is *not* you, it is the affair of the intelligence. [In English Maharaj said, "You . . . No!"] Now I am talking in English.

Q: The English language is blessed.

M: My teaching is spread among all the foreigners through the English language. Very intelligent people, very advanced, thousands of them. The beauty lies in the fact that my knowledge will be in conflagration in foreign countries. It will be spread in America and from there it will be spread back to the Indians. When the Indians receive it they will say, "It

---

[4] *Mountain Path* (Tiruvannamalai, S. India: Sri Ramanasram)

has the approval of the foreigners, therefore we will accept it."; that is the nature of the Indians. Indians are like this. If somebody goes to America or England and works, even washing dishes, when he returns many people will go to see him and present garlands; that is our nature.

Q: Ramana Maharshi was a great sage, he was unknown in India. When Paul Brunton wrote the book in English about him, everybody went to see him and he became well known.

M: I agree with that. Ramana Maharshi was discovered by Paul Brunton and I was discovered by Maurice Frydman.

July 19, 1980

Maharaj: In this spiritual hierarchy, from the grossest to the subtlest, you are the subtlest. How can this be realized? The very base is that you don't know you are, and suddenly the feeling of "I Amness" appears. The moment it appears you see space, mental space; that subtle, sky-like space, stabilize you there. You are that. When you are able to stabilize in that state, you are the space only.

When this space-like identity "I Am" disappears, the space also will disappear, there is no space.

When that space-like "I Am" goes into oblivion, that is the eternal state, *nirguna,* no form, no beingness. Actually, what did happen there? This message "I Am" was no message. Dealing with this aspect, I cannot talk much because there is no scope to put it into words.

Questioner: Does Maharaj go into samadhi?

M: I am stabilized in the Highest. There is no going into *samadhi,* or coming down from *samadhi;* that is over.

Q: Should we continue our meditation?

M: It doesn't mean this is an excuse for you to give up meditation, you must persist in meditation until you come to a stage when you feel there is no meditation. When the purpose of meditation is gained it will drop off naturally.

Q: Which is the way to the Supreme state?

M: There is no question of going into that state. You *are* the Supreme state, but whatever ignorance you have will drop off.

I've been advised by doctors not to talk, therefore I am not talking.

Q: Is there a desire not to die and lose your body?

M: The sage is not concerned with that.

Q: Is there a desire of the body, not of the Self?

M: You may say something like that; this is the administrative action of that beingness.

It is a very complicated riddle. You have to discard whatever you know, whatever you have read, and have a firm conviction about That about which nobody knows anything. You can't get any information about That, and about That you must have firm conviction. How difficult it is.

Most people reach that state which *is,* but nobody reaches that state which is *not.* It is very rarely that one can reach that state. It transcends all knowledge.

Most essential is that knowledge "I Am." Claim it, appropriate it as you own. If that is not there, nothing is. Knowledge of all the stages will be obtained only with the aid of this knowledge "I Am."

From the Absolute no-knowing state, spontaneously, this consciousness "I Am" has appeared — there is no reason, no cause. Spontaneously it has come, with the waking state, deep sleep, the five elemental play, three *Gunas,* and *Prakriti* and *Purusha.* Then it embraces the body as its self and therefore identifies as a male or a female. This "I Amness" has its own love to *be:* it wants to remain, to perpetuate itself, but it is not eternal.

This passing show may be likened to the following situation: suppose I was well all along, then suddenly I was sick and the doctor gave me medicine. After three days my fever was gone. So this stage of fever for three days is the "I Am" consciousness. Exactly like that — a passing show, a time-bound state. This principle loves to be, and one must not belittle it — it is a very Godly principle. This "I Amness" contains the entire cosmos.

It is said that all this is unreal. When is it certified as unreal? Only when one understands this temporary phase. And in the process of understanding one is in the Absolute and from there recognizes this as a temporary, unreal state.

In my present state I am not able to talk much. The difficulty is that you have been accepting this as real and I have to disprove this and a lot of talking is to be done by me, which I am not in a position to do now. So, you go now, do *bhajans.*

July 20, 1980

Maharaj: You are having experiences in the world with body and mind, but what do you know about your identity? You have an image of yourself, but that identity is only a temporary thing.

Questioner: What is mind?

M: Mind is the language of the vital breath. That mind-language will talk only about the impressions it has collected. The knowledge "I Am" is not a thought but observes the thoughts.

Out of *prana,* the *pranava,* the beginning of sound, in the sound is the love to be. The innermost, subtlest principle is that gnawing principle "I Am, I Am," without words, by which you know you are. It has no form or image, it is only beingness, the love to be.

Para shakti is the beingness or love to be. The next stage of the *para shakti* is *para shunti,* the formation but not yet perceptible. The next stage is mind formation: the language is formed in the mind, next is the explosion of words, vocal words. In this where are you? This is a process happening.

For you I am expounding very secret knowledge about your own beingness, how it came about — that is what I am talking about.

This play is just happening; you are not playing a part. When you are ignorant, you think you are playing a part in this manifest world. There is no one working deliberately — it is happening spontaneously. You cannot claim anything in this process. When you are thoroughly knowledgeable you will come to the conclusion that this beingness is also an illusion.

Q: Who recognizes that it is illusion or ignorance?

M: Only that one recognizes or witnesses all that as ignorance. That one cannot understand That one, he can witness and understand only the ignorance. The one who recognizes all this as ignorance, that one is knowledgeable. Why are you calling me *jnani* and listening to my talks? Because I have recognized and understood that child ignorance, the "I Amness," and have transcended that.

Finally you have to understand that the principle which you are using to talk, to move about, and operate in this world, is not you.

Q: I have read and listened to so many stories about the different sages and personalities of the past, and they were all different, they founded different sects, etc.; why is this so?

M: According to the time and the situation they have taught their concepts, but they are concepts meant only for that period, that situation,
and then their concepts have developed into religions.

All of you presume that you are very knowledgeable spiritually.
Before you think of deriving any benefit out of anything, first of all, find
out what is your identity.

July 21, 1980

Questioner: Why did I take this form?

Maharaj: Because you were a fool. If you had known anything about it,
you would not have come into this world.

Q: First I hadn't any form, isn't that so?

M: Yes, even now you don't have any form. It is not your shape, it is the
shape of the seed.

Q: Isn't it the nature of the seed that it grows, like a tree grows out of a seed?

M: It is its nature.

Q: So, I am not to blame. The seed must be foolish.

M: Because the seed is foolish it has come like this. The seed is the original foolish state, yet what big titles are given to that seed. The seed is
transient, and the whole world is full of the seeds. All the five elements,
all the objective world, is in that seed. You are not the seed — you are
the observer of the seed.

For many centuries the Western people were not interested in spiritual matters, but now they have realized that, in spite of all their riches,
they cannot get real peace, so they are searching for the truth now. The
nearer you get to the truth, the more you lose interest in worldly affairs.
Such a one will not have any particular interest in the world, but will act
like an ordinary person.

The sum and substance of spirituality is nothing but to come to a
decision, make a judgment, about the Self, God and the world — what is
it? You must first dispose of this question.

This world is filled up with selfishness due to your association with
the body. Once you know what these principles are, then you dissolve
the personality, and in the process that selfishness vanishes because you
are no more an individual.

Q: How can I be in my true state and lose my fear?

M: You are already in your true state. Because of the mind, duality comes in and therefore you are afraid. The association with the body and mind is because of love for the body-mind; that is going to go away, therefore everyone is afraid of death.

Q: The world is given to me by my senses. When you go beyond that state of "I Am-ness" do you experience the world?

M: There is no question of going beyond. I was never born, will never die. Whatever is — is all the time. Going beyond is only an idea meant to remove all other ideas you have accumulated. You think about birth. Do you know anything about your birth?

Q: No, I do not know that I am born. I feel that I am really not born, and yet the world seems so real.

M: Do not worry about the world. First start from here: the "I Am," and *then* find out what is the world. Find out the nature of this "I."

Q: Why find out about the "I" which is not real?

M: It is the seed from which everything comes out. If the seed is not there, the universe is not. How have you come into this so-called objective world? Here everything will be wiped out. I invite you, in your own interest, to go home.

July 22, 1980

Maharaj: All these discussions are an exchange of ideas and mental entertainment, meant to while away the time.

Questioner: If you don't make some kind of effort, you get nowhere.

M: Don't think that some progress has to be made. You will continue to do something, even if it is conceptual, but the one who understands that he is already there, what will he do?

Q: Okay, but isn't there tremendous scope for self deception here?

M: Who is this who is going to be self-deceived?

Q: The empirical ego.

M: There is no entity. It is not possible for a phenomenal object to achieve something, and this is only a phenomenal object.

Q: Don't you have to make that effort to stand back?

M: Not doing anything means what kind of doing?

Q: Our normal way of living is identifying. If we stand back, is there a qualitative difference?

M: Carry on your entertainment, but don't be under the misapprehension that you are doing anything.

Q: When I say that I am God, how come people don't come and prostate before me?

M: If you have truly understood that you are God, before that conviction comes you will have lost your identity, you will have merged with the total manifestation, therefore who will expect whom to come and do *pranams?*

Q: Is there such a thing as using one's will to do something? If one is trying to stay awake, saying a mantra, *or meditating, and keeps pulling himself back from sleep, is he not doing something?*

M: At the stage of a seeker what he is doing may be right, but he will soon find out that the seeker disappears in the seeking. When the seeker disappears there is no question of doing. Later the seeker will understand that it was not his true nature which was doing all this, but that to which the label "born" was attached — that is the consciousness which has identified itself with the body and the states of waking and sleeping. That whole bundle is what was doing and he is not that. This body is perceptible, but my true nature is That which was *before* the body and the consciousness came into being. Anything that is sensorially seen and interpreted by the mind is an appearance in consciousness, and is not true. I am not telling you anything which is foreign to my experience, I am telling you what I have understood and experienced. It is very simple: this is time-bound and anything which is time-bound is untrue, because time itself is a concept.

What I am telling you is based on this simple fact, as it is based on my experience. If it appeals to you as a concept at the moment, accept it. Otherwise not.

If at all you want to do something, do that which you cannot do at all. That is the state of no-being.

Q: There is a constant restlessness in the mind, wanting to realize something; that in itself seems to be an obstacle.

M: Are you prior to the mind or after?

Q: Prior to the mind.

M: So don't worry about the mind. Employ your mind to the extent that is useful for your normal daily chores, not beyond that.

M: The knowledgeable one just witnesses or cancels whatever experiences are obtainable through the mind as having no substance. All this world play is in the realm of the mind; once you understand that you are not the mind in what way are you concerned? This is a temporary phase, imperfect, inadequate.

Q: *Even beingness is an imperfect temporary phase?*

M: That consciousness is a product of the food essence body; the body is the fuel on which "I Amness" is sustained. Do you not observe what the body is? Is it not a morsel of food and water? Presently you are embroiled in this "I Amness," but you — the Absolute — are not this "I Amness."

Q: *What you are saying is, even the "I Amness," the way you recognize it in the mind, that is not the way it is actually?*

M: Take it like this: this is as good or as bad an experience as having a tummy ache or a pain in the neck. In my perfect state I never had a pain, but when the "I Amness" was there, suddenly I felt the pain. That "I Amness" will merge, will disappear, I am the perfect state when "I Amness" was not. I definitely know that "I Amness" was not. Just as I have to suffer a chronic ailment I suffer this beingness. Just understand at what level I am talking, to what level I am leading you.

Just imagine the flight to which this spiritual talk has gone. The normal spiritual approach everywhere is to worship this consciousness with so many titles, but to me it is a pain and I want to get rid of that.

July 23, 1980

Questioner: *Maharaj says all that is necessary is to be aware. The mind keeps on casting doubts, and particularly keeps on saying that there must be more practices or something more to be done.*

Maharaj: All the activities are in the field of consciousness, the mind, and vital force. The knower of the mind is just a witness. It does not interfere in anything.

Guru's grace means the knowledge you *are*. When you stabilize in this conviction, that will open up and give you all the knowledge and that is the grace.

If you are there, then everything is immeasurably there. You give no significance to the fact that you are — you are carried away by all the manifestation which is the expression of your beingness.

Q: My tendency is to look outward, rather than inward.

M: That is the quality of your "I Amness," not of you, the Absolute. You have embraced the body as your Self. That also is superficial, you don't know what is happening inside the body either.

Q: Correct. I don't know what's happening in my organs or how they act.

M: All the actions happening in this wide world, the samples of all those, are also happening in the body.

Q: That which is, does not know Itself?

M: In that state you do not know you are. With the tool, or aid, of beingness you know you are.

Q: With the tool we try to go beyond?

M: Don't try to go beyond consciousness, only recognize, understand, what the beingness is, that does the trick. The proof that consciousness was not lies with you only. You, the Absolute, are the proof of that. Spontaneously, uncalled for, this beingness has come and this beingness is being witnessed by you, the Absolute. Ask questions — you will not have such an opportunity again.

Q: The urge is not so much to ask questions, as to just be with Maharaj.

M: That is quite proper. Just by sitting here quietly and listening to the talks you mind will be annihilated. In case the mind sprouts again you forestall it by asking questions.

The mind is sprouting, expressing itself with various concepts. Don't identify with that, let it go. Don't be a customer to your mind concepts.

Q: Things like getting food, eating at regular times, earning money, all these are concepts of the mind and are responded to by the mind. If one does not respond to these things, then how does one live?

M: By all means employ the mind, but don't get lost in the mind. Observe the mind, be a witness to the mind flow.

July 26, 1980

Questioner: I have come to Maharaj in the hope that he may help me put an end to this search.

Maharaj: Can you communicate to me what you have understood?

Q: It is all concepts, all illusion.

M: Yes.

Q: I don't believe in processes that take time and disciplines, I've done all that. I want it to end.

M: The basic fact — that you are not the body — must be clear to you by now. You are working in the world and you think that you are doing that work, but what is really happening is this: the life force, when it comes out in thoughts and words, *is* the mind, so it is this *prana* mind, life force mind, which is the acting principle. The beingness, the consciousness, is the God which witnesses the life force and mind working. It does not interfere; it merely witnesses. The reason for your unhappiness is that you think it is you are working.

Q: I realize that anything I say is a concept arising out of my consciousness.

M: That you are, and the world is, are both concepts. You must know that.

Q: How does this knowledge work? I mean: you tell me words and there comes a sense of understanding. Is it a mental process? Is there still a faculty witnessing all this?

M: The mind understands because of the consciousness.

Q: Then it is all an automatic happening?

M: That is true. The mind interprets whatever the concept is, the base is consciousness on which the concept arises at the moment.

Q: So what is there actually to attain if you cannot change this consciousness and you cannot touch, cannot reach by words? It is there all the time, right now. So for what are we here? Doing belongs to the mind — that is clear — it is going on like an automaton. I see clearly now. I want this mind to surrender to the consciousness. Do you understand?

M: All this conceptualizing, all this articulation, has been taking place only after the original concept arose that you are . What was the position before this concept arose? At that time did you have any concepts, any needs?

Q: Like deep sleep?

M: This concept that it is like deep sleep is not incorrect, but it is still a concept, and the original state is beyond concepts.

Q: What is the fact now?

M: That you are awake is itself a concept at this moment. Let this sink in.

Q: It's a movie.

M: Go back to the source: before this concept of beingness, "I Am," arose, what was your state?

Q: I don't know.

M: That which you don't know, that is the right state. Everything that comes after this consciousness is attained, is like a dose of salts — it is useless, consciousness is useless.

Q: So the search, all aspects of it, belongs to the same?

M: Throw away every thought, every experience, everything that happens after this consciousness has come. Other than throwing it away as useless, there is nothing to be done beyond this firm understanding in which you become more and more absorbed.

August 1, 1980

Maharaj: All your worldly and unworldly activities are based on the individual identification. You, as an individual, want to have liberation. You remain as an individual, that is the difficulty.

However much you may think you have understood this knowledge, so long as you think that you, as an individual, have acquired that knowledge, the individual identity is still there.

One who has made certain progress which gives him some tangible results is a Yogi, but because his self identity is there he rests content with what he has achieved as an individual.

You must understand both the aspects of this beingness, this lowly physical nature from which it has arrived, and that at the same time there is no end to what this consciousness can do although this state is by nature limited. How can he who is aware of his true nature and the total potential be satisfied with anything that this limited state can give him?

Further, the potential of his abiding in the Absolute is so great that people are not able to imagine how it could be in the Absolute, what it is like — therefore they can only think of him in his consciousness state.

Questioner: How can one understand that we abide in consciousness?

M: Right now you are in that state, but you always try to judge through body-mind. You are still attached to the body-mind. Even if you might live for a hundred years, you would still like an extension of five years. In the Absolute there is no need of any kind, even the need to know oneself.

Q: There must be some cause for this temporary state arising out of the Absolute?

M: Because of the friction or interaction of the five elements this temporary phase has occurred. For example, there were two intimate friends, whose friendship had endured for a very long time, but suddenly there was some friction, some disagreement, and immediately they had a fight.

Q: At the time of death there might be a very traumatic experience, physical and mental.

M: It is not always so. For the one who has purified the mind of all concepts, to that one death will be very blissful.

You have had a lot of learning and spiritual wisdom and still with all this, at the moment of death you will open your diary wherein you have noted all your relatives.

Q: With your blessings I will have a peaceful death, I will not remember anybody.

M: Abide in the high state. You have to do nothing, only the listening. If you listen correctly, everything will happen. Now I have told you what this beingness is, it is the outcome of the five elemental play; that knowingness is the result of this food body, and you are not that. So why worry about the departure of the knowingness?

Have you understood that you are the witness of the consciousness that appears on you? You are not the consciousness, you are not the knowledge, *sat-guru* is your true nature.

Consciousness cannot be separate from the world and the universe, it is the same. This is my *maya,* it has come out of me, and I know that I am not the *maya.* I am the witness of this, it is just my play, but I am not the play.

The final meaning of all this *sadhana* is you. Whatever is, you are. Nobody has written these things in the books so far, some people may write hereafter. One who would write on this should have a scientific outlook.

That knowledge which appeared on me, I pampered excessively, and what is the final fruit of such knowledge? That knowledge has been branded now, "You have a disease and now you are going to go away," so I know the nature of this knowledge which appeared on me. You find out for yourself. I danced with that knowledge, I called it God, and now this knowledge has been branded as sick — but I know what I am, I am prior to this. I complained to my own nature, and my own nature says it is all *lila* (play), you have nothing to do with it. The very consciousness is dishonest, what have I do with it? I am the support — people think I am the cause but I am not the cause, I am the support.

Q: In the jnani *beingness has reached the state of no-beingness, still the appearances will happen, how will one act?*

M: It is something like acting in a dream world, in the dream world everything is happening, you are not doing anything. From that highest state only witnessing of the beingness and the activities of the beingness happen.

August 8, 1980

Questioner: Should we have a firm conviction that there is a state beyond the consciousness?

Maharaj: The Absolute is there is any case, so there is no question of your having faith — it is there.

Q: Would a firm conviction change the consciousness into the Absolute?

M: There is only one state, not two. When the "I Amness" is there, in that consciousness you will have many experiences, but the "I Am" and the Absolute are not two. In the Absolute the "I Amness" comes and then the experience takes place.

In the Absolute there is no individuality, no memory that I am this or that, but there is continual stirring.

I have nothing to say which can be termed as hearsay, or which has been read, or has authority from the scriptures. What I have to say is coming out of my own Self.

Whatever is happening, from the Absolute standpoint, without the knowledge "I Am," is very profound, unlimited, expansive.

In the realm of beingness the fragmentation begins; it is limited, conditioned, because in this beingness we try to claim all the actions as ours.

In the Absolute I have no occasion to say that I exist, because It is in eternity. I do not have to make any comments about my existence. Because of the existence of the Absolute *Parabrahman* state a lot of incarnations have come and gone, but the Absolute remains untainted by the movement of all these incarnations.

Q: What is the purpose of the creation?

M: This is the language of the earnest seeker, not one who is established in the truth. Out of an infinitesimal seed a magnificent tree has grown; will the seed reject the tree, the branches, the leaves, etc., asserting that this is not me, not mine? Spontaneously, it is going on. Let it go on.

Q: Is this "I Amness" a necessary threshold to obtain that Absolute state?

M: The Absolute state cannot be obtained. That is your state. To the Absolute state the witnessing of the consciousness happens.

Q: How long must one practice?

M: How long did you practice to become a woman?

The first stage is to transcend this body-mind sense, it is easy, but to transcend consciousness is very difficult. Beingness is a very powerful potential knowledge, because of that you have all other knowledge, therefore it is difficult to get rid of this knowledge.

Q: Is it separate from the Unmanifest?

M: From your point of view it is separate; from my standpoint it is not separate. Sri Krishna said that whatever is, is myself only. *Saguna* and *nirguna*, both myself only. This touch of beingness is a temporary phase. Enquire at that point. How did this beingness happen to be?

August 21, 1980

Maharaj: I am not very keen on having people stay longer than eight or ten days, whatever they have understood, they have to digest, any further talks will not reach them.

Presuming that one is knowledgeable, having left here and gone elsewhere, he will not be able to remain alone — he will crave somebody's company so that he can deliver the goods of spirituality. He will want the company of others with whom he can discuss spirituality — otherwise he will feel very unhappy. Will you feel happy and satisfied if you do not encounter other *sadhakas?*

Questioner: Oh yes. Is this a necessary threshold for a serious seeker — to go through the stage where he would like to share his knowledge with others?

M: That is part of it, but that must also come to an end. The highest state is the unborn state in which there is no experience of mind. Investigate that concept "I Am." In the process of trying to find your true identity you might even give up the Self, and in giving up the Self, you are That.

[Maharaj is watching some sparrows on the windowsill.] The consciousness indwelling the sparrow and the consciousness indwelling this body is the same. Here the instrument is big, there it is smaller. They [the sparrows] are planning for food, their tummies are not full. All the species are suffering; creation itself is suffering. All these concepts about rebirth, etc., has the rain rebirth? the fire? the air? In short, it is a mere transformation of the five elements. You may call it rebirth.

In the process of this spiritual search, all will happen in the realm of this consciousness. You finally stumble on, or culminate, into the Absolute *Parabrahman* state, which is desireless.

I have understood and transcended beingness. Suppose I live for 100 years more, waking state, sleep and "I Amness" — what is the use of that? I am fed up with that.

I don't have any exclusive identity for myself. Whatever identity I have is the play of the five elements, and it is universal. Since there is not much that can be said from my state, I will not be keeping people long. I will just dole out some knowledge and tell them to go. With this profound knowledge, at this level, they are not able to understand. What benefit can they derive?

August 23, 1980

Maharaj: Some people I will request to stay but I can't explain why, and some people, although they would like to stay, I say, "you go." There are various types of seekers: some come exclusively for knowledge and are not interested in the person who delivers, perhaps least interested in him. Some people want knowledge, but for them the prior requisite is *gurubhakti,* devotion to the guru comes first; after that they collect knowledge. There are some great sages who, in their seeking stage, used to do devotion or worship of a God only for name's sake, but the intensity was devotion to the guru and because of the intense *gurubhakti* they reached such a high state.

Now, for this lady, devotion to the guru is predominant, and she gets knowledge incidentally, but starting with *guru bhakti,* to such a person even the God is devoted.

Whatever natural experiences you encounter, just accept them, don't try to alter them, just accept them as they come.

The sum total of all this is illusion and nobody is responsible for crea- tion — it has come spontaneously and there is no question of improve- ment in that — it will go on in its own way.

I have come to the conclusion that the world is there spontaneously without any seed, that creation is seedless but the world is full of seeds and procreation is going on daily.

Questioner: Having knowledge, how is it that you have been able to deal with all these different persons?

M: Who is to deal? I have no pose or stance, no set form of my own. If I had a set form, it would have been difficult to accept or coalesce with anybody, but my nothingness is the subtlest, so I can fit into anything, any situation.

Suppose a rich man, wearing a lot of expensive ornaments moves in the street, he will be afraid, he will be in danger. But a naked fakir has nothing to lose, so he moves in the streets without fear.

So, having lost everything, I have nothing further to lose, I can en- counter and fit into any situation. So long as you wear a name and form, all these problems will be there. In this spiritual pursuit you gradually lose your form and as the form is shed off, the name also disappears.

There are many customers to gain and possess something in the name of spiritual knowledge, but nobody is a customer for the real, true Self knowledge.

There was a man who worked hard and gathered possessions for many years and now he is on his death bed in his village house. On his death bed he was looking into the cattle shed, he was not thinking noble thoughts, he was looking at the calf who was chewing a broomstick, and he was worried about the damage to the broomstick. So, even when he was dying, he was shouting, "The broomstick, the broomstick!"

Q: What is the yardstick to measure the progress of a seeker?

M: There was a very weak man who was not able to walk. Gradually he acquired strength and started walking, so he knows that he has the strength, isn't that so?

The indication of your progress is your disinclination to associate with normal people; your desires and expectations get less and less. When out of intense hunger for Self knowledge, the door, or the floodgate is opened, then you start rejecting everything, right from the gross state to *Iswara* state, your own consciousness, you reject everything.

In worldly life, by the power of money you can purchase anything, by donating money you get everything. Similarly, by donating the Self you get the Brahman and when you donate the Brahman you get *Parabrahman*. You must have a deep, intense desire for Self knowledge.

August 24, 1980

Questioner: If chaitanya *(consciousness) is all pervading and consists of all these powers of various kinds and yet, the individual consciousness is connected with the body, for this universal consciousness is there a body? A universal body — or a combination of bodies for the universal consciousness?*

Maharaj: Universal consciousness does not have a body. The universal consciousness becomes manifest whenever a body comes into the picture. The essence of the five elements constitute the sustenance of the universal consciousness.

Q: The universal consciousness and the consciousness in the body, does it have any connection?

M: It is an intimate connection. It is a continuum from the individual consciousness to the manifest consciousness. For example, you have the vital breath: outside it is called universal air and when you breathe, it is your *prana.*

Q: What is the difference between Paramatman *and* Jivatman?

M: When you think in terms of parts, you think of *Jiva,* and of the whole as *Paramatman,* but there is no difference. When it is entrenched in the body it assumes a temporality, a time unit, the *Jiva;* at the end of the time span it merges into the *Paramatman.*

Q: Why does Paramatman, *which is whole, limit itself to the body as a part?*

M: There is no reason for it, it just happens. But in the *Paramatman* there is no awareness of existence, there is awareness of awareness only. As soon as awareness of existence comes, there is a duality and the manifestation comes.

Q: Earlier someone said that man alone can realize. I feel that every living cell is a manifestation of God and therefore that this is a wrong idea.

M: The consciousness is the same, but the mind can only work according to what is known to it. What is known to the lower creatures is only the basic physical requirements. It is only man, who from an early age, has been thinking of, and has been fed, higher ideas, other than merely the physical aspects. Man is able to fly and go to the moon. No other species can do this; the mind of the lesser species is limited.

There are 84 lakhs of different species, as soon as any conception takes place in any of these species, there is a sort of a causal body on which the print has been made at the time of conception about the nature of the form and its working. Nobody tells a bird to fly, a fish to swim, or a worm to crawl, it is all in the conception itself. That which cannot die is now firmly convinced that it is going to die. How has this fear of death crept in? It is based on the concept that one is born, on mere words; this is the bondage.

All that one has to do is find out one's source and take up headquarters there.

August 29, 1980

Questioner: After knowing that one is not the beingness, the beingness still wants to be — it protects itself. Is it built into that unit?

Maharaj: Yes, that is its nature.

Q: Is it that these units of beingness are of no more value than a picture, they are just like a picture on a TV screen — is that right?

M: Yes, you may take it that they are just pictures. Nevertheless it is a most amazing instrument because inside it has a certain principle which contains the universe. Don't just dismiss it as a picture.

The Self cannot experience its knowingness without the help of the body. It is a necessary instrument. Sour food and pulsation (vital breath) — without these the growth is not there and beingness will not be there.

This body is a bag of nourishment but that knowledge "I Am" is not individualistic, it is universal.

Q: Is it the consciousness enjoying itself through all these units of beingness?

M: Yes. This beingness goes into individuality because of the form of the food package, the body. From my standpoint it is dynamic, manifest beingness only — no individuality.

Once you take to this understanding there is no question of enjoying yourself as an individual. You are no more an individual, the individual is dissolved. A rare one will do this.

The one who has understood all the five elements and its play is not worried about the essence of these five elements, the beingness — this state is transcended also. That one has the fragrance of humanity: he remembers humanity, but knows that he has nothing to do with humanity.

Having understood this and transcended it, the words are of no use.

The beingness feels that it should not die, but if the so-called death has occurred, there is no loss to it.

From my standpoint, whatever beingness in the form of a human being was there is all gone; because of that dissolution it has become manifest.

August 30, 1980

Questioner: Does the consciousness remain forever?

Maharaj: No, the consciousness is there only so long as the body is there.

Q: Even when one understands, will there be bodies coming into existence and dying?

M: Yes. The five elements, three *gunas, prakriti* and *purusha,* together are the means of demonstrating the "I Amness."

In the original state there is no sense of consciousness, no awareness of being, but as soon as the "I Amness" comes the entire manifestation is seen at once, this is the expression of the consciousness. In the Absolute the "I Amness" is whole but the expression is in many. I manifest Myself in many. Human beings are one type of form and each type of form will act according to its nature, according to the combination of the three *gunas.* How can an individual come in?

The only way to understand this mystery is to realize your identity with the universal consciousness, which is expressed in the total space. So long as you identify yourself with the human form it is impossible for the mystery to be solved.

Why do you come here and waste your time for an hour or so? If you do some physical or mental work for two hours you would have something to show for it.

Q: These are the hours that are useful; all the others are useless.

M: How can they be useful? I am destroying that for which you say these two hours are useful. I am destroying the identity.

Isn't it amusing that the teaching which destroys the individual is exactly what the individual wants? The answer is that there never was an individual. The knowledge comes that the individual was never there.

Q: What is the realization?

M: Before the idea "I Am" sprouted, you are, but you don't know you are. Subsequent to that there have been many happenings with which you have started decorating yourself. You try to derive the meaning of yourself out of subsequent words, happenings, and the meaning of words . . . that is not you . . . give it up. You are prior to the idea "I Am." Camp yourself there, prior to the words "I Am."

September 11, 1980

Maharaj: Whether one be a *jnani* or an ignorant person his bodily nourishment, sustenance, maintenance, etc., goes on through the meaning of the words of his mind. His thoughts will also flow according to the impressions he has received since childhood. The activities came out from the vital breath, the words, and the knowingness "I Am."

If you want to invoke your Deity you will have to worship the vital breath; through the vital breath you approach your Deity. The image of any God is given through the vital breath. the language of the vital breath means *words.* When all aspects of the vital breath are purified there is no scope for desires, there are no physical or mental sufferings. As per the command of the Guru hold on to the "I Amness" — the *Atman prem* — I love." All our activities, physical or spiritual, are based on emotion. All these details I accept, but I know that the sum total is zero.

My earlier talks anybody could understand, to some extent, but my present talks are very difficult to understand. To become qualified to understand, stay put at that source of your birth.

The talks are spontaneously flowing out. I am not framing them. I myself am often amazed as to why these types of profound expressions are emerging, and people who listen to my talks are also nonplussed because they are not able to frame any questions based on my talks. Everything is spontaneous, the stage of witness also has come spontaneously. All my activities come out spontaneously, there is no scope for thinking.

Since I know my state prior to birth, I also know that birth point, and since the birth, whatever I am — my beingness — I also know. That's why I talk like this. The experiencer and the experiences, both are to be dissolved. The moment the translators come and I take my seat for talking, I am energized, my battery is charged — otherwise I am down and out and have to use this cane. I am least inclined to collect any spiritual seekers of any grade.

Questioner: *We can understand with our mind but beyond mind we cannot understand.*

M: From deep sleep to waking state, what is it? It is the "I Am" state with no words, later the words start flowing and you get involved with the meaning of the words and carry out your worldly life with the meaning of those words — that is mind. But before this "I Am" and waking state, that borderline, there you have to be.

It is only a rare one who understands what I am driving at. To a normal spiritual person we have to say, "You do this or that and you will get this benefit." Then for the time being he feels happy and relieved, but this is not final; he again comes back to the same cycle. But we can't help because he has no capacity to understand the subtlest aspect of this spirituality.

At the most, I would say, "You know you are; you worship that 'I Am' principle. You worship that, be one with that only, and that 'I Amness' will disclose all the knowledge." That's all I will say, but the subtlest part is this, from deep sleep to waking state. To abide in that you must have an intensely peaceful state. In that state, witnessing of the waking state happens. You must go to that limit, but it is very difficult. For a normal person, with the arrival of the "I Am" and the word flow, he will go with the word flow. The one who has discrimination, who is intelligent, and is intensely spiritual, we must bring here prior to that "I Amness."

If you have regard for me, remember my words. The knowledge "I Am" is the greatest God, the Guru; be one with that, be intimate with it. That itself will bless you with all the knowledge relevant for you and in the proliferation of that knowledge it will lead you to the state which is eternal.

You will become mature enough to be in the province of that *nirguna* (without attributes) state. You cannot convert a raw mango into a ripe mango, full of juice, overnight. It must pass through the course of time to maturity. Is this clear to you or not?

September 15, 1980

Questioner: In meditation when I try to stabilize at the point behind the mind, there is darkness, nothing, blankness. I don't like the state.

Maharaj: Don't you see — You are still there. Prior to stabilizing in the Self, traces of the mind are still there.

This machine is a self-generating machine; when you go into that the momentum helps clear all doubts in your mind. This is exclusively your knowledge which you will enjoy most, and then all traces of the mind are completely uprooted. This is the stage where you are — you are not, that is the borderline. The moment you know you are duality is there, when you do not know you are, you are perfect, but you must go through this process. In deep sleep you do not know you are, but that is a grosser state. In this alive state you must recede into the state of no-knowingness.

What is this knowingness? It is the stamp or registration of the booking "I Am." You are booking a flat which is under construction but where is that flat? It is only the booking. Similarly this "I Am" is only booking, it represents your Absolute state.

Q: What gives you the courage to transcend in the nothingness which you know is there?

M: Your deep urge to understand the Self. Receding only means to go within, your normal inclination is to come out through the five senses and see the world. Now reverse; I am not the body, I am not the mind, I am not the senses; now you are stabilized in consciousness. After stabilizing in consciousness all further things will happen automatically. You expand into the manifest.

I was, I am, I shall be in that original state before the "I Amness" came.

Why is it that the terrible name of this disease has no effect on me? For the simple reason that what I am has nothing to do with that of which the disease is just a name.

Q: What does Maharaj think about all the different religions?

M: As far as I am concerned all religions are based on concepts and emotions. Those emotions are so violent and absorbing that people have immolated themselves.

Being one with some other personality emotionally can be so effective that those who have identified themselves with Jesus Christ have had the marks of crucifixion appear on their own bodies. All these experiences are totally useless. One individual has identified with another individual, and unless individuality is given up the Reality can never manifest itself. Do not repeat what you have heard, parrot-wise, unless you have it with the conviction that I have.

I know my state before the body and consciousness came, I have the knowledge of it, I have the awareness of it.

Merely listening to these words will not do — you must be one with the consciousness. Don't treat that knowledge "I Am" as insignificant, because it is the stimulating force for your entire universe.

The expressions of consciousness are limitless; if you enter into the expressions you will be lost. Surrender to and be one with your consciousness and your consciousness alone will show you the process of how it can be dissolved.

September 21, 1980

Maharaj: All that one does is for the continuance of the consciousness, but for me there is nothing at all that I would like to continue.

You come here as individuals expecting to get something from me, that is where the mistake arises. There is no individual, so how can I do something for a non-existing individual? Your true nature is in no way different from mine. This happening is just a happening which has come and which will go.

If one feels he has to urinate, he just has to urinate, it is not something different for each one, it is a process of urination which happens to everybody but you consider everything as something happening to you as an individual.

Questioner: How can I understand what Maharaj is saying?

M: Discrimination is very necessary to understand what I am saying. It is only after the arrival of consciousness that we try to understand ourselves. Consciousness is the so-called birth; birth means the three aspects: waking state, deep sleep and the knowledge "I Am." Once I understand what this birth is, then the whole mystery is solved. Since I have thoroughly known what this birth principle is, I will know very well at that happening of the so-called death, I shall observe the departure of the vital breath, the language and the "I Amness"; there is no question of death.

If I understand right now that my vital breath is quitting, I am not going to arrest it, I am not going to say "You stop now, wait for some time," because I know very well it is of no use retaining this vital breath and life force.

Any number of dissolutions have come and gone, but in my true, eternal state I am untouched by them. Prior to this experiential state I was perfect in every respect, with the arrival of this beingness this imperfect state has started, and I am fed up with that.

If you really want eternal peace, don't bother about anybody else, worry about your own self, investigate only your own self.

Who is going to give you eternal peace? It is only that sun, that "I Am." If you embrace that Self-effulgent sun everything else will go, but you will prevail eternally.

Investigate fully. With what authority can you sustain yourself? To what extent can you prolong your life? You should realize that beingness is not independent — it depends on something. When you investigate you will come to the conclusion that you, the Absolute, do not depend on that beingness.

Q: If Atman *is* sat-chit-ananda *(being-consciousness-bliss), what is* Paramatman?

M: Sat-chit-ananda will, in due course, become the *Paramatman*. *Sat-chitananda* is "I Amness" and is itself a state of bliss, a state of love, but it is an experiential state, so long as consciousness is there, and consciousness is there so long as the body is available — it is a time-bound state. You must transcend the *sat-chit-ananda* state.

Q: Should I stabilize in beingness or should I flow with the thoughts?

M: If you stay put in beingness the thoughts will get less and less. If you get mixed up with the thoughts they will multiply. Stay put in beingness only.

September 24, 1980

Maharaj: How many years back did you take the *mantra* from me?

Questioner: Three years ago.

M: The knowledge you are is God. You worship that and one day you will realize that you are not an individual. You will realize that you are the universal consciousness which cannot suffer; there is no pain or pleasure for that consciousness. Not through intellect, but through intense meditation you will know it.

The meditation will be done by that consciousness itself. To meditate on something is to become that.

I am fully established in that unborn state but still I am experiencing this state of multiplicity, but it has no effect on me.

Q: What is the effect of being with the Maharaj?

M: Presently the effect on the seeker is more. If you have the purity it is faster, for the impure and dull it is slow.

I didn't know I was, presently I know I am, this is the same "I" with the knowingness mantle over it. This is the way the very Absolute transformed Itself into this grosser consciousness state, the state of appearance. I am the God, I am the devotee, and I am the worshipping; all the same, one common principle.

Q: Was the saint we were speaking of, who was so irritable, a jnani?

M: Yes. *Jnani* means knower of the knowledge.

Q: How could he be so irritable if he was a jnani?

M: In the manifest consciousness all the activities are happening, so-called good and bad. In the manifest consciousness this quality was expressed. You cannot attribute this *tamasic* quality to a *jnani* because he has transcended the individual consciousness.

Q: Is it all right to eat non-vegetarian food?

M: So long as you feel that you are an individual you have to abide by the code of conduct given to you. Once you are the manifest consciousness there is no question of *do's* or *don'ts*.

In the universal manifest consciousness is there anything good or bad? Nothing of the sort. The fragrance of flowers will be there, garbage will be there; it is all the play of this consciousness. The witness of the consciousness cannot come in the realm of the consciousness.

Q: Suppose the witnessing stops, is it samadhi?

M: Suppose you all go away, there is no more witnessing, I am still here, but I have nothing to witness. In that beingness the otherliness is there and witnessing takes place. If consciousness is not there the Absolute cannot know Itself — there is nothing but the Absolute — therefore no witnessing.

Q: Suppose I am just watching that all actions are happening through me and I am doing nothing, is meditation necessary?

M: That is a sort of meditation, but the right meditation is when you meditate on your Self. You come to that state when you woke up in the morning and you watch the consciousness; that is the state when you meditate on your Self.

Presently you think that consciousness is watching consciousness, but consciousness is being watched from the Absolute platform only.

September 27, 1980

Maharaj: All this spirituality is only for understanding your true nature. To achieve this what is "being alive" is the whole question. Once you know your true nature then being alive is not as an individual but being alive is simply being a part of that spontaneous manifestation. There is nothing to be sought, the seeker is what is to be seen. Merely see the picture as it is.

All of you are seekers: let me know what it is that you are seeking.

Questioner: Can you reach that, not just by meditation, but by living with others in the world?

M: Unless you are part of the manifestation can you live? Know this! When you are not conscious, your world does not exist. You are conscious of your presence and the world outside, they are not two things. Understand this. The world can exist only if this psychosomatic apparatus is there. If you consider this apparatus as yourself, you accept death and die. The *jnani* knows this to be just an apparatus and is apart from it.

Having understood this, you do your job happily. What is happening is spontaneous and all activity is part of the total manifestation.

Q: If manifestation is spontaneous, is there any reason, or cause, of all actions?

M: In dreams you live for 100 years but when you wake up that dream lasted for just five minutes. How did that happen?

Q: Does Maharaj relate the causeless happening to that dream?

M: The basic reason for all this great cause is that you exist, so find the nature of that. All these acts are done by the child of a barren woman. All these are problems of the consciousness; find out the root of the consciousness.

Q: How?

M: Catch that consciousness by the throat. Conceptual consciousness by conceptual throat. Pamper and woo this basic consciousness, it alone can satisfy your quest, not your intellect. Unless that knowledge is pleased, you cannot have knowledge.

I never knew; if I had the slightest knowledge would I have descended into the prison of my mother's womb? Whatever happens, happens by itself. Who can have knowledge of that which existed before conception?

There is nothing to be acquired. You are That.

September 28, 1980

Questioner: Why so much attraction of the "I Amness" for the body?

Maharaj: When it expresses itself as "I Am" it is already fully charged with that love to be. Why, in the insect, worm, animal, or human being, this instinct to keep itself alive? Because with the sprouting of the life force, this "I Amness," that is itself the very instinct to live, to love to live. That love to be is the prime motive force for all life's activities.

You will find, when you are the manifest consciousness, you alone are the multiplicity; you express yourself in all this ample, manifest world. This state will itself be transcended, and you will be in the *nirguna* state; but these are all your expressions, only you as "I Amness."

What I am talking about now is more subtle and more profound and very difficult to understand, but if you understand the job is done.

Consciousness is an aid to know. Presently that consciousness knows itself as the body, it should not be so, consciousness should know consciousness bereft of body sense.

Understand logically what I have been telling you again and again. This "I Amness" is the outcome of the food which I eat. Am I the food? No, I am not; the outcome of the food I also am not.

All will realize this knowledge, but presently you are caught up with this intimacy with the body.

"I Amness" has no authority of its own; it is a puppet in the play of the five elements; it is an outcome of the five elements.

The one who expresses "I was not," Its position is secure and stable and eternal.

Whatever you witness will not remain with you. It is imperfect. The One who recognizes the imperfect is perfect, It is total, It has not to do anything for Itself because it is perfect and complete in Itself.

Why can the *Parabrahman* afford to have this luxury or suffering of this manifest world? Because to the *Parabrahman,* this does not exist.

September 30, 1980

Questioner: Oh, when will I understand what Maharaj is telling us?

Maharaj: It will come gradually, because of all the concepts. You have to get rid of those and that takes time.

Some people are in search of knowledge which is acceptable to their mind and intellect, but the sphere of the mind and intellect is of no use to receive this knowledge. All your experiences and visions depend on your knowledge "I Am" and this itself is going to dissolve.

For this knowledge there are no customers, no devotees, because they want something concrete in their hand, but when your knowing-ness itself is going to dissolve, is it possible to hold on to something?

Your guru tells you that you have a true identity, but it is not this. It is formless, *Parabrahman.* That *Parabrahman* is without any doubts. It is not conditioned by *maya,* because with reference to *Parabrahman, maya* does not exist.

When you listen to this you feel satisfaction and with that the matter ends for most people; they don't meditate on this again and again and try to find out that principle behind everything.

When will I be pronounced dead? When the *Atman* has left the body, but I am not that *Atman,* where is my death there? I am not affected by cancer because whatever happens, whatever the experience, I surrender all those to the *Atman.* All the actions and fruits of the actions are sur-rendered to the *Atman* by the *Parabrahman,* the Absolute.

You can never have knowledge about your Self because *Parabrahman* cannot be witnessed. You know what you are *not* — what you *are* you can-not know.

October 1, 1980

Maharaj: The Self is subtler than the space. There is no birth or death for the Self.

Don't accept what I tell you blindly; ask me questions. Thoroughly scrutinize and examine the knowledge which I expound and only then accept it.

You live in the house but the house is not yourself. Similarly, the knowledge "I Am" is in the body but it is not the body.

Questioner: *I do not fully understand it.*

M: With the mind you will never understand. You are not the mind, nor the words, nor the meaning of the words. I expound the knowledge of the Self to the Self but you accept it as the knowledge of your body.

I am completely detached from the body and the consciousness which is within the body. Nevertheless, because of the disease, the unbearable suffering of the body is being experienced through the consciousness. It is unbearable but since I am detached both from the body and the consciousness, I am able to speak to you. It is something like the fan — the breeze is there and the sound is also there. In the same way the vital breath is there and the sound is also emanating, but all this happening is unbearable. . . the suffering has to be endured.

When the knowledge "I Am" is not there do you perceive or observe anything? Knowingness is knowledge and no-knowingness is also knowledge, but it has no form. If you equate it with the body, only then you say that you are a male or a female.

In the absence of knowledge, the question of I know or I do not know does not arise. When you understand what I have said about knowledge you will fully identify with that.

Spontaneously I have realized that I am written off from the book of consciousness. You will not feel happy unless you taste yourself through your body. The body has importance only because the "I Amness," the consciousness, is dwelling therein. If the "I Amness" or consciousness is not there the body will be disposed of as refuse.

Call that knowledge "I Am" as your Self, don't call the body as knowledge.

Normally the Gurus will not introduce to you the Self so deeply. They will only introduce to you all the rituals.

The knowledge "I Am" is the primary God; meditate on that only.

Presently, one may ask why man has created a God. The concept of a God is, if you pray to such a God, that God will give you whatever you want. Such a God is great. We have an idea that if we demand something of Him he will give it.

October 2, 1980

Questioner: I want to give up this ego, but I don't know how.

Maharaj: What is the measurement and the color of this ego that you want to give up? What have you understood about this ego?

Q: It is a false conviction of the mind.

M: It is a pinch in my fingers, this "I Amness," but all the scriptures, the sixteen *sastras,* eighteen *puranas* and four *Vedas* have been screaming and shouting, trying to describe this Brahman. All those praises are only for that tiny little pinch "I Am." The moment you start making a design of that "I Amness" you are getting into deep waters.

This incense holder is silver, you have the knowledge that it is silver. What is the shape, color, or design of that knowledge? If all knowledge is formless, could there be a form, design or color to the knowledge "I Am"? Could it be subject to sin or merit?

In this timeless ether the touch of "I Amness" is not there.

Q: Is it not true that out of compassion for the ignorant the jnani *expounds knowledge?*

M: You can say whatever you like. There is no such thing as compassion in that state. I have elevated you to that state where you should know that you are the very illuminant of everything, and the love to be is also therein. When I lead you there why do you ask me such questions? How do you know anything?

Q: Through the mind.

M: No. The knowingness recognizes the mind, the mind cannot recognize consciousness.

You are overpowered by sleep, you wake up — who recognizes this? Prior to mind, the knowingness principle is there. Prior to knowingness, there is the priormost principle which knows the consciousness.

In the final analysis out of the absence of knowledge, knowledge was born and knowledge delivered the world, all beings and all things.

The one who enters spirituality is like cold water which is put on the fire. When you put it on the fire the bubbles start rising and in due course it starts boiling. That boiling stage is something like the *sadhaka* entering the highest class of spirituality; at the boiling point he likes to talk a lot, put a lot of questions. When the fire is applied continuously the boiling stops and simmering takes place. That is the stage where one acquires knowledge in spirituality. After listening to these talks will you be able to go into quietude? I have my doubts about that, because you still like to please your pampered mind. If you have really understood what I say does it matter if you please your mind or not?

I have told you that presently you are like that warmth in the body. What is the *Parabrahman* like? The *Parabrahman* does not experience this warmth of "I Amness" at all. If you understand, this puzzle will be solved for you.

After understanding this, if one becomes a *jnani,* that consciousness principle and body is available, and they will be involved in the emotional field also. It will give full vent to crying and it will also enjoy whatever situation is there. Such a *jnani* is not going to suppress any expressions of emotions which spontaneously come out of this consciousness and body apparatus.

Normally people suppose that a *jnani* should suppress all the emotional outbursts. That is not correct. With your standpoint in the Absolute, you are not concerned with the feelings and instinctive outbursts of the apparatus.

A *jnani* does not volitionally participate, it is spontaneously happening; while an ignorant person is deeply involved in that, he assumes everything is real. For the *jnani,* the warmth is also unreal, so whatever happens in the realm of warmth is unreal.

All devotion, liking, and love, is dissolved for a *jnani,* but whatever he does is for others.

October 4, 1980

Questioner: *What is the difference between my state and Maharaj's state?*

Maharaj: For the *jnani* there is no difference. The difference arises in the case of the ignorant because he is still identifying with the body. Give up the identification with the body and see what happens.

Q: *How?*

M: I can only tell you, "this is it" — how to accept it is beyond me and I have no remedy for that. I tell you but you must understand it.

Q: *Once and for all: if we take his words literally is this all that is necessary?*

M: Yes. That is the one to be caught hold of, but what is the instrument with which you will catch hold of it? It is not the body, mind, and intelligence.

Q: The will?

M: Any effort you make will land you in further trouble. Therefore it is for this knowledge that you exist — to accept this knowledge, not the pseudo-identity. Just keep what you have heard from me in mind as true, and then act in whatever way arises spontaneously.

My Guru told me that I am timeless, spaceless, without attributes. Then I decided that if that is the case why should I have any more fear? Who is to have fear? Suppose you meet a tiger: the tiger is going to eat you in any case, therefore there is some chance that if you attack the tiger it may run away, so why not take that chance? Why not try and disidentify yourself from the body? Whatever unhappiness you have, whatever fear you have, is based entirely on identification with the body. Make an effort gradually to disidentify yourself from the body.

It is a simple thing. Death is inevitable, so why don't you accept what the Guru has told you, that death is something which cannot affect That which you are. This identification with the body is time-bound; why not disassociate yourself now?

How many of you will remember and understand what I tell you? Whatever fear you have is based only on memory, concepts, and hearsay. So long as you cling to any concept or memory this fear will not leave you. Don't protect this fear — give it up, let it go. Can you do it?

You have been accumulating what you have heard from me, but ultimately, whatever is accumulated has to be given up. It is to be understood, used, and then given up.

Q: Maharaj says that everything has happened spontaneously but we are accustomed to thinking that everything must have someone to start something, someone to control. Without this controlling authority it is difficult to imagine anything functioning.

M: In the state of duality this idea has to be there, otherwise there can't be any concept or any functioning, this is the basis of manifestation. When ultimately the knowledge merges in knowledge, the seeker disappears and there is no one to ask questions.

What is being said and what is being heard is time-bound — from a particular time until today — but That which we are is totally separate from that which is time-bound.

I can understand and measure this time duration, so I must obviously be separate from this duration.

October 8, 1980 (morning)

Maharaj: All knowledge is available through the body, but this knowledge which you are, which is an outcome of the food body, is not you.

This beingness itself is the love. It is most natural and therefore I love all others because I love myself. The fountain of my love for others springs from the love to be.

The Unmanifest is manifest through that waking, dynamic, manifest spirit; that is the state of love to be. The wife is not devoted to the husband, she is devoted to that love to be.

You have an earnest desire to be living in the body but you have to dispose of this body. Just as you eat delicacies and the next day you have to evacuate it as fecal matter, in the same manner you have to dispose of this body. My own condition is complete manifest consciousness and the expression of the body is only the sum and substance of the vital breath, the language of the vital breath (the words) and the love of Self.

There is no other thing like *Paramatman* except "I Love." In that ecstasy who is going to look at the body? Body becomes irrelevant. How many titles have been given to it, but what is it . . . only that love for Self.

Always, forever, your knowingness has been moving about, but you have limited it to your own body, and therefore you are killing it. *Paramatman* is not *maya,* it is your real nature.

Questioner: What should one do about one's daily duties?

M: You should attend to your duties — they are not personal, they are of the manifest consciousness, they belong to all.

Try to expand yourself to Infinity as the manifested consciousness. There is no other God but you.

One day this body will drop dead; people think that death means completely unmanifest, but it is not so, it is not like that. When something is consumed or exhausted, it becomes more, it becomes manifest.

Sri Krishna said, "I reincarnate myself at every *yuga* (eon)," but I say, every moment I expand, ever more I am created, I proliferate more and more every moment.

I never seek anything from anybody else. Whatever I want to get, I want to get out of my own being. I worship that very principle "I Am" and demand what I want out of that; because of that, all these things are coming.

His Majesty the Emperor has gone to sleep — it doesn't mean he is dead. You are not able to realize this knowledge because you hang on to the body. Only a Self-Realized Guru can direct you.

Without this body sense I am perfect, total, complete. You will not be able to comprehend my talk.

October 8, 1980 (evening)

Maharaj: What is the cause of the waking state, sleep and "I Amness"?

Questioner: The chemical.

M: When you utter that word — "chemical" — do you consider yourself to be that?

Q: I have studied that chemical thoroughly and I am not that. Everything is contained in it but it is not me.

M: Just as this flame is the quality of the burning of the gas, similarly, because of this chemical, there is the experience of the waking state, deep sleep and knowingness; they are not your qualities.

Various names are given to the chemical, *mula-maya, sutra pradam,* etc. It is all illusion. There is no God, no individual soul, nothing.

The primary illusion expresses itself through Self-love, love for beingness. From deep sleep you wake up; similarly the disciple who considers the words of the Guru as final, and follows his words and does accordingly, remains like that. Ultimately he gets the knowledge of the Self. Just as you wake up from deep sleep, you get that knowledge "I love"; Self love, it merges into the *Parabrahman* unknowingly. When you meditate you and that Self love should be one — there should not be any duality.

The main problem with *jnanis,* those who intellectually have this knowledge, is their attachment to their relations and their belongings.

Nobody *dies,* death means *finished;* for example, a drop of water when it evaporates has become infinite. There is no death for anything, everything finishes to become infinite.

The *purusha* is that principle from which everything flows, all the manifestation; it is the support for everything. When you know something, you have to become that; in order to know the God you have to become that. In order to know that *purusha* you have to be that.

Q: Maharaj was speaking earlier of attachments, what about attachment to the Guru? I find all other attachments are gone but this remains.

M: What do you mean, attachment to the Guru? You and Guru are one, not two.

Q: How am I to follow what Maharaj says when I have so many things to care for —family, etc.?

M: Your consciousness alone is taking care of everything; look at your consciousness as God. The first thing you do after waking up is to meditate on that consciousness, that "I Amness"; worship that consciousness for some time before you start your daily activities. Before you fall asleep at night, again abide in that consciousness, "I Amness." Be devoted to that, and in such a mood go into sleep.

That consciousness which meditates on the Self, that Self will be revealed to you.

People worship so many Gods, but these Gods are only concepts which have occurred to the mind.

People say they want to save themselves; save what? What are you trying to save?

All your knowledge is dissolved here, so you can have no pride of being a *jnani* when you leave here.

October 14, 1980

Questioner: In the presence of the Maharaj I feel there are no more questions.

Maharaj: You feel that the doubts are dispelled, still the day is far off, just wait.

Q: Can Swamiji suggest one thing so that we may enjoy eternal bliss?

M: I have a very simple remedy, and that is that I am not the body. Had the world been real, there could have been some treatment — but it is not real. Whatever you do is of no use. Everywhere you see all this chaos, in spite of all efforts. You cannot stop it — it is in a continual state of flux, and it is all unreal.

After listening to my talks do you acquire and store knowledge, or is whatever knowledge you had being dissolved?

Q: Becoming dissolved. Can I carry Maharaj to my home?

M: I am just like the city of Bombay; can you carry Bombay home with you? This experience of the world is happening to you spontaneously, not out of your efforts. Even your understanding of the Guru must come spontaneously. Nothing will stop — all the process is going on without your effort — so many bodies are being created and dying. All actions for the running of the world are already happening. The process of creation of millions of bodies is already going on in the space. Out of the weeds, the grains have come, in those grains the "I Amness" is latently present. That phone message, "Hello, I Am, Hello, I Am," is already there in that grain of food. If you create something out of your own efforts, only then can you destroy it — but this creation is not your effort.

October 15, 1980

Questioner: There are many moments in my life when I don't like the situation and I want to change it.

Maharaj: You may fight with the situation but you are not the situation.

Q: When you start watching the mind you know that you are apart from the mind and you would not like to get involved with the fight of the mind, so naturally the friction will become less.

M: In this process you, as an individual, are not left at all. Try to understand that "I Am" is a product of the *satwa guna,* food essence product.

The friction is the fight between that quiet witness and the world. The fight began when the words began emanating from the consciousness. Words have come out of you and you embrace those words; you become the champion of the meaning of those words which have come out of you.

You have a mountain of concepts and words. To get rid of these you use other concepts. When you throw out all the concepts, including your primary concept, then whatever is, is. Stay put in quietude.

Q: Are words necessary or is it just the presence of Maharaj?

M: No doubt association with a sage is conducive to realization, nevertheless it must be followed up by questions and answers. There are always some doubts arising from mind, so until all traces of mind are removed you must clear them out by words.

Q: These days, when thoughts come, I just turn away, I feel I stop them now.

M: If you can do this it is all right, but if they are flowing, let them flow.

Q: Not being involved in your thoughts — is that enough?

M: Yes, that is the only thing, and whatever has to happen will happen; the very doing you have given up.

Q: So, it is no more necessary to try to change yourself, to try to do better things?

M: When you don't hang onto thoughts, you are no more a person.

Q: It makes me a little scared. Everything can happen — I can do crazy things.

M: This is a common stage, all people go through this. Fear is a quality of mind and mind does not want to lose itself.

Recite the *nama-mantra,* hang on to the *mantra,* because this is a stage where the mind is losing all support, therefore you give it the support of the *mantra.*

Q: The things that I don't like in myself, they derive from a thought as well, so I can let go of them also?

M: Yes. Don't say *myself,* that is also a thought.

Q: So in the end it is as simple as that: it's just getting rid of thoughts — it's true.

M: It is not a small achievement. You may feel that you are thought-free but at some stage thought will pounce on you suddenly. Many so-called sages, although they attained that thought-free state, still had their fall.

October 17, 1980

Maharaj: Just be as you are, don't imagine or picturize. Your body and your image have changed continuously all during your life and none of these images has remained constant.

After twenty-five years your body will give up this image and will have an old person's image; later on that image also will go. If these images had been real they would have remained; they are unreal. The "I Am" principle has no form, no color, no design. Through these designs we enjoy or suffer, but nothing is real; any experience you get is not real. Whether you are crying or laughing, this is the image for that moment only — the next moment it will be changing. Some people are very good at weeping, crying, lamentation, only for that moment.

So long as the body is there this passing show will be there, continously changing, and finally, that very consciousness through which you see the world will quit. The days are numbered of this body and consciousness.

Questioner: *If I have not fully attained when I die, will I have another birth?*

M: If you go with that concept, that concept will have another birth. You don't know what form that concept will take.

Only that person will be visiting me whose destiny is being fully exhausted. Nothing of his destiny will be left.

You are a lady from some far off country, why should you be visiting this place? Because your destiny is being annihilated.

November 7, 1980

Questioner: Consciousness is time-bound, so whatever I am, is it also time-bound, or is there not something which is eternal?

Maharaj: So long as the body is there you are this consciousness, but once the body and the consciousness go you are that original state upon which all this has come as a temporary state. Your original state is changeless and permanent.

The difficulty comes because you are all searching for That, forgetting that That is what you are. You, as the subject, are seeking you as an object. You are what you are seeking.

The moment there is a pose, there is fear. Anyone who has assumed the pose of a seeker will be bound to follow the traditional practices of a seeker, and the limitations.

What is the purpose of all that I am saying? It is a direct attack on identification with the body-mind. So long as that identification is there my direct attacks will continue.

Once dis-identification with the body-mind takes place, Brahman will come with folded hands to your feet.

Q: Does this dis-identification take place suddenly or gradually?

M: It depends on how you look at it. If you are waiting for it, it will be gradual; when the last step is taken it is sudden. When it does happen you will realize the identity of the non-manifest and the manifest; they are one, there is no difference.

The true knowledge can only come when all possible concepts have been given up, and can only come from within.

Parabrahman has no beginning and no end, It is eternal, whereas this consciousness is time-bound — it has a beginning and an end.

Just as you wake up in the morning and come to know that you are, similarly this has happened. Because I am, I woke up, if I was not, how could I have woken up?

Parabrahman comes to know that It is, the consciousness is how *Parabrahman* knows that It is. *Parabrahman* is your eternal state, you cannot remember it because you have not forgotten it. It is your dail· experience, you know it. There is consciousness, there is no question oi I"; It is.

The life force is in the grain in a dormant condition. Understand that life force and do not condition it to any form. This beingness is not something which you can capture a handful of, it is manifest — like space, it is all over.

All this profound talk is nothing but mental entertainment. As you go further into spirituality you will realize that "I Am" is the very God or soul of an infinite number of universes, but that "I Am" is again entertainment. All my talks are conceptual entertainment.

November 10, 1980

Maharaj: Up to what point in the past can my memory go? I was a small child and I remember riding on the shoulder of someone, an elderly person; he was taking me on some hill and I could see the sun rise — that is my first impression.

Have you even given a thought to this? At what age did you get the knowledge of your own body? Suppose you started knowing yourself at the age of four — whatever actions took place prior to the age of four happened without your knowing and there is no record in your memory of that. You have heard from others of things that happened, but you directly do not know. There is a scar and it is said that I was bitten by somebody, but there is no memory of that. So many things happened before the child knew itself.

In the first few years the primary concept "I Am" was there, but in a dormant condition. Later on it started knowing itself.

The *jnani* state is like the child state, when the child was not knowing itself. The apparatus through which that knowingness expresses itself is now quite different, but the principle is the same.

The *jnanis* will have different ways of expressing. Ramana Maharshi used to wear only a loin cloth, just washed, not ironed — but here, I would like to see that there are no wrinkles, very neat.

There was another great Sage who was not conscious of his body; he used to move about naked. Lord Krishna was also up-to-date, like me, and very well dressed. People get lost in the external expressions of a *jnani* and try to imitate that instead of going to the presiding principle.

Now I thoroughly know that very first moment, I know what is birth, everything I know, nevertheless, could I volitionally enter into that birth? What doership or authorship did I have, to enter or not to enter, or to decide anything? When I say that I got the knowledge of my birth, do I really know directly what happened at that moment? This is all conceptual knowledge; also all knowledge since then is conceptual.

November 11, 1980

Maharaj: There are Sages or Saints abounding all over, but they still aspire to be, they would like to continue their beingness.

How long should I continue this waking state and deep sleep, waking state, deep sleep? So long as this cycle continues the knowingness also will prevail there. Have you encountered anyone who was tired of this waking state and deep sleep state? In the waking state you carry out a lot of activities, and when you are tired you fall into sleep. In this continuous cycle what is the advantage?

Questioner: It is said "Rarely somebody appreciates the skill of God." What is that skill of God?

M: Where is that God? If you want to inquire about some skill, inquire about the skill of your parents.

You have created a God because you want to beg from somebody and that is what you call spirituality.

Q: I don't believe in that kind of God. I believe that God is that touch of "I Amness," as Maharaj says.

M: If you really understood and digested what I have said you would not set foot in this place.

Q: If I have understood what you have said there is no need for me to come — it's all right — but let me ask you, factually it is like . . .

M: What do you mean by facts?

Q: Even to understand that what should I do?

M: Do that thing which you can't do.

This world of *maya* is built up of concepts only. I cannot charge the world with giving me the pain; the whole cause of the pain is this knowingness "I Am." When this knowingness was not there, was there any pain or pleasure?

If you want to encounter God, dive deep into your own Self; that is the very storehouse of everything.

Q: How does the dream state happen?

M: In deep sleep there is an apparent waking state in which that "I Am-ness' feels itself waking up and creates a dream world.

You know very well how you proceeded into this mess. You inquire into this and keep quiet.

After listening to my wildly virulent talks you may not come tomorrow, it doesn't matter. I tell you again and again, you might run around and around the world, but nobody is going to give you the knowledge. Recede into your own Self. Surrender to your own beingness and that alone will give you all the knowledge necessary for you — no one else will. You don't inquire into this, you blindly follow the rituals of spirituality.

You may be anywhere, but be honest, be devoted only to your being.

November 23, 1980

Questioner: *Is the witnessing done by That which is prior to consciousness, or does consciousness witness itself?*

Maharaj: Cross that bridge when you come to it. Don't worry about the principle prior to consciousness, you just be the consciousness.

Q: Are Gods only concepts?

M: Gods means consciousness only. Collect whatever you can in the absence of consciousness.

Q: We are not able to understand the state of a jnani. *If the* jnani *has become one with the Absolute, where is the scope for the display of consciousness? We don't understand how a* jnani *can be* Parabrahman *and be here also.*

Translator: A *jnani* can transcend consciousness and be the Absolute on demand; he can come into consciousness because that particular body is still available — through that body communication takes place with the beings in consciousness.

The example given in our scriptures is like this: You have an ocean and the water from the ocean in a pot, now that pot is dipped into the ocean, the pot is still there, but the water in the pot merges with the ocean water, so that water does not feel any difference, but the water in the pot can also witness the pot. It has the advantage of being one with the Absolute and to use the body also. With this example I am able to understand what the state of a *jnani* could be.

M: Understand beingness and all will be solved. It is all your speculation about that Absolute state from your grosser state. Presently it is like a signboard indicative of the *Parabrahman.* The word *Parabrahman* is not *Parabrahman.*

Your habit is to ask questions. A few words are flung at you, some concepts are given to you, and you say that you understand.

The only theme of my talks is you — you know you are. How and why do you know you are? It is only about that which I talk.

You have no authority over this consciousness, it has come by itself and it will go by itself. You can't do anything with it.

Q: *The whole idea of control is meaningless then?*

M: Yes. You have absolutely no authority over it.

Q: *The very foundation is taken out from under us.*

M: All your moments of spirituality are based on the "I am the body" idea. This knowledge "I Am" is going to remain for a short period.

Q: *What about those who say they are the incarnations of this one or that one? Are they just ideas?*

M: This will be very clear to you when you remain in your real position. Until then, accept it if you like. Until you know your true state you will accept all these hearsays because you don't know the truth.

You need not go to that prior state. Presently, what you are — this primary concept — thrash it out. When you thrash it out, what you are prior to the concept is open. Normally, a *jnani* will not explain in such detail to a seeker.

You have thoroughly studied the teachings of Ramana Maharshi. In his teachings did you come across this aspect?

Q: *The more I listen to Maharaj, the more I understand the teachings of Ramana Maharshi.*

M: Have you understood Ramana Maharshi?

Q: *I can never understand, because he is the Absolute, not an object to be understood. I am not an object either.*

M: Yes. Ramana Maharshi is the Absolute, you are also That. The Absolute cannot be caught in the domain of your experience. Are you convinced?

Q: Yes.

M: Why did this beingness of mine happen? What was the cause? You must get to know what this is thoroughly.

Q: What is the point of trying to find out answers to these questions? Is it not sufficient for me to know that I am, that my beingness has appeared and will disappear? Why do I need to know all this?

M: You must know! The knowingness is the outcome of what? The quality of what?

Q: It's a quality of food.

M: Oh yes, but when do you come to know of it?

Q: It is not my experience.

November 29, 1980

Questioner: This that I am — and the consciousness which is time-bound — what is the relationship?

Maharaj: What is the concept of "I" with which you are trying to find a relationship? This is exactly where the misconception arises.

In this concept of space and time there is total manifestation, in that you consider that you are something separate. There is nothing separate, you are part of the function of the total manifestation.

As Absolute, I am timeless, infinite, and I am awareness, without being aware of awareness. As infinity I express myself as space, as timeless I express myself as time. Unless there is space and duration I cannot be conscious of myself. When space and time are present there is consciousness, in that the total manifestation takes place and various phenomena come into being.

I, by Myself, Awareness, descend into this consciousness, and in this consciousness I express Myself in manifold ways, in innumerable forms. This is the crux, the framework of manifestation; there is no question of any individuality.

What is this? [Holding up a bag of apples] There is no difference between this fruit, a goat, or a human being. They are all food products, all three are food.

All creation, every creature, is made up of the five elements, and the behavior of each creature depends on the combination of the three *gunas, satva, rajas, tamas.* There is no question of being responsible for anything that happens in the world. It is only by taking delivery of responsibility that one suffers.

The consciousness of being present, the five elements and the three *gunas,* that is the total of the universal manifestation.

In your original state there is no awareness of awareness, therefore no question of knowledge. The knowledge comes only with the appearance of the body and consciousness. This knowledge is really ignorance, and whatever knowledge is based on that is also ignorance.

You have been practicing spirituality for many years, what do you have in hand?

Q: I am consciousness, that is my profit.

M: Is this profit permanent? Is that your true nature?

Q: I identify myself with the total manifestation.

M: All that, is it not only after you got your consciousness? Go back to your state before this consciousness came upon you.

First you identify with the body, then you identify with the consciousness, after awhile you continue to be the consciousness, but the trap is that you will think you have become a *jnani.* Even being in consciousness is time bound. The original state is before the consciousness came upon you. In one case the knowledge was given, it was understood, and the person became That in one day; another took a thousand years, and also reached that state. Is there any difference?

What was originally something which I loved, now I no longer want it because I am aware of my true nature. I no longer need this consciousness, even for five minutes.

At the end of your life you will be prepared to pay five lakhs of rupees for an extension of even five minutes. I am not prepared to give even one rupee. I have lost all love for this manifested world.

M: You must maintain this knowledge "I Am" in proper order. I quarrel with my people if they don't keep these utensils in proper and clean order. Suppose this towel is left unwashed — then I will play hell with whoever is responsible. All the dirt which is not the towel should be removed. Similarly, "I Am" is the tool through which you get all the knowledge. You worship that "I Am," remove all the adulterations, the dirt.

Q: How to worship the "I Amness"?

M: That knowingness alone points out all the dirt which is imposed on it. Even the space is not as pure as the knowledge "I Am." Innately the world is very pure; it is rendered dirty because you identify with the body. Since you do not recognize your "I Amness" in its purity, you refer to various books and Sages to get an identity.

Q: (another) I am afraid of losing my beingness, my existence.

M: Where is the question of worry? Even the *Parabrahman* does not know Itself. When we come to the conclusion that you are not, I am not, what is left is said to be *Parabrahman,* but what is *Parabrahman?* You can't describe it, so you are silent. I am also silent. *Parabrahman* cannot be compared with anything.

Q: Is Nama-Japa *useful?*

M: By all means do it and its worth will be proved in due course. You have to abide in that *japa;* it is no use conceptualizing what benefits you are going to derive from it. Follow it and realize the benefits. Even if the one following *Nama-Japa* is like a donkey or dud, he will become a great Sage — that power is there in the recitation of a *japa.* When that person comes across a *Sat-Guru,* the Sage tells him, "You need not take care of yourself because you are that immanent principle "I Am." You need not take care of anything. You just be and everything will be taken care of for you."

It is a pity that you depend so much on hearsay and you don't try to investigate for yourself. Your knowledge is confined to your body and borrowed knowledge.

All the activities of the world are going on because of this "I Amness." It is the source which creates the world. Understand that "I Amness' first — only then can you transcend it. First of all, be that "I Amness."

November 30, 1980

Maharaj: This "I Amness" is a function of nature, a product of the five elemental food body. It knows itself, it loves to be. With the aid of this knowingness, get to know your Self.

Many eons have come and gone, but no person could retain his identity or his memory perpetually — it is gone with the departure of the body. The five element essences, plus the three *gunas,* means a person; with that this knowingness comes, the memory "I Am." This personality is sustained by the provisions supplied by the five elements. So long as the provisions are supplied in proper order the body and "I Amness" will be there. Once the supply is stopped the touch of "I Amness" is gone.

That which has come to see Maharaj, do you recognize that? Is it the body, or something outside the body?

Questioner: Inside or outside, I don't know.

M: Very good reply. Keep aside the body and describe that.

Q: I can't describe it.

M: Since you can't describe that, what is the use of that?

Q: No use.

M: Once you understand this, you will get the truth. The one which is listening, which you do not know, is you, and the one which you know as you, you are not.

The highest purpose of spirituality is the *Paramatman* — that knowledge that indwells the body, "I Am," and that cannot be described. When you firmly agree that this is right, does it not mean that you have the spiritual wisdom?

Q: Who can get spiritual wisdom?

M: Except you, who could that be? You and you alone. Who could ask "who am I" but you? If the questioner "I" is not there, who is going to ask questions? This is the culmination of spiritual knowledge for you; you need not come again.

Q: I like to be with Maharaj.

M: You can sit here. Now whether you live one year or a thousand, the result will be this only.

Q: Maharaj answers my questions before I ask them.

M: Initially you accept what other people say but in due course, whatever is accepted is thrown overboard.

Q: I cannot have any experience of how beingness came into being because I have no knowledge of what existed before being.

M: This knowledge is very simple and, at the same time, very profound. Who will know all this process, the appearance of the knowingness, and finally its disappearance? The one who understands this reaches the state of *Sat-Guru,* but an ordinary person cannot understand this. *Sat-Guru* is not the child of human parents.

To know these secrets, to understand these secrets, you surrender to that very principle "I Am," and that consciousness alone will lead you to this. Presently, stabilize in the consciousness. If you don't do that, your very concepts will be very dangerous to you — they will throttle you to death. The knowledge you are is the source of all energy, the source of all Gods, of all types of knowledge.

Having heard these talks, you need not come again, you have only to abide in that conscioussness you are, that very dynamic principle because of which everything is. Stabilize yourself therein. Confirm your stability there. You are only that. This is the simplest method: you know you are, just be there.

December 7, 1980

Questioner: I want direct experience of the Ultimate.

Maharaj: The Absolute cannot be experienced. It is not an objective affair. When I am unicity then that is pure awareness which is not aware of its awareness, and there can be no subject and object — therefore there can be no witnessing. Any manifestation, any functioning, any witnessing, can only take place in duality. There has to be a subject and an object, they are two, but they are not two, they are two ends of the same thing. When consciousness stirs, duality arises. There are millions of objects, but each object, when it sees another, assumes the subjectivity of the Absolute, although it is an object. I, as an object, perceive and interpret all the other objects, and I assume that I am the subject, and the witnessing takes place.

Q: Why does consciousness stir? What is the cause?

M: Without any cause, spontaneously, it happens; there is no reason. That consciousness is universal — there is no individuality. But when the consciousness stirs in a particular form which has also arisen spontaneously, and starts functioning in that form, that form assumes that it is an individual and what is unlimited limits itself to a particular form and the trouble starts.

Let us say that someone has become a *jnani*, but what was it to begin with? It was that sour, bitter, principle, that secretion because of which the consciousness has taken place. That very principle, the knowledge "I Am," has developed, grown, and become sweet; it matures and becomes the manifest *jnani* state; but what is that? It is the product of the five elemental food essence. When that goes, what remains? The Absolute which does not know Itself.

Q: The desire for liberation is also a desire, isn't it?

M: Don't talk about liberation, talk about yourself, what you are. When you understand that, both knowledge and ignorance disappear. You only require knowledge so long as the ignorance is there.

A knowledgeable person can tell anything to an ignorant person to remove his ignorance. For that purpose he takes the aid of the so-called worldly knowledge, concepts, and both the worldly conceptual knowledge and the ignorance go simultaneously. A *jnani* will give you any concepts to remove your ignorance. This "I Amness" is the knowledge and you are embracing that. To remove that he gives you all these concepts; to understand that you are not this "I Amness" which is an outcome of the food essence product. Once you realize that, whatever concepts he has given you, together with this "I Amness," are to be thrown out. What remains is the Absolute.

This is the actual state of affairs. You can never say I am like this or that — you are without knowledge. Rarely will one understand this and transcend the domain of consciousness.

After listening to my talks, you think it is all very simple, but it is not that easy.

December 9, 1980

Maharaj: Here you will get to know what is, not what you expect to hear. Duality arises when consciousness arises. I am present and I know that I am present — that is duality. I am and I am not conscious of being present — that is unicity. There is only one, but when this conscious presence is there, then there is a sense of duality.

Questioner: Is a Realized person aware of everything?

M: Actually no one is realized, there is only pure knowledge. It is only for reasons of communication that we say a person is realized. The knowledge has realized that it is knowledge; that is all that has happened. I am not the body, I am not the words; when knowledge recognizes this it is called Self-Realization.

Q: The knowledge Maharaj is giving is for jnanis. What happens to the very simple man who is not able to comprehend this?

M: *Bhajans* and meditation. By meditation the knowledge which is immature will gradually grow into maturity.

Q: *A thousand years ago people were primitive. They could not have understood this. It is only for developed minds.*

M: Whether primitive or civilized, people can understand this. Even in those days there must have been some to whom this knowledge did appear and they instinctively understood.

This knowledge is not new; it has always been in existence. People came to know instinctively.

Q: *Why is it that India seems to be the cradle of this knowledge? No other country seems to have this knowledge.*

M: That is not so. This manifestation is the expression of the Absolute, and the manifestation may take various forms in various countries. Where it takes what kind of expression is immaterial; basically all is the manifestation of the Absolute. There is no cause and effect, no reason why one thing should be in one place and something else in another. What is to be found out is what one is, by oneself.

Q: *Can the Guru give a push toward that knowledge?*

M: You think that you are one individual and the Guru is another individual but that is not so. Guru is the knower of this consciousness, which is temporary.

Understand this curious situation: while I am talking to you there is unbearable pain in the body.

I have understood firmly that there are no individuals separate from one another, no knowledge separate as worldly knowledge and spiritual knowledge. There is no Guru and no disciple, there is no God and no devotee. There are no opposites — they are a polaristic duality, not two separate parts, but two parts of the same one. I am convinced of that and yet I am talking to you. You accept it as knowledge and I give it as knowledge. Understand this amusing factor.

The talks emanate spontaneously out of me; prior to the emanation of the words there is no meaning fabricated inside. There is no part played by the mind. It is direct spontaneity.

Q: *What is the definition of consciousness as used by Maharaj?*

M: Consciousness, as it is used here, is this sense of being alive, of being present, the sense of existence. It is the love of being that is the source and cause of all desires.

December 13, 1980

Maharaj: The Absolute is unicity, by Itself, but it is expressed in manifold ways and forms. As Absolute I have no experience of myself. The devotion without another is devotion to the Self, where there is no duality. Once the duality comes, the devotion is divided between subject and object. Before birth we were not conscious of ourself; only when a foreign element, the birth, was introduced, did we become conscious of ourself.

Apprehending this is awakening and for this there is no path or technique. This is so subtle that I would like to speak more about it, but it is physically impossible for me to speak more than a few words.

What I speak about openly, others will not. The amount of receptivity each one has depends on his own luck. Understand also that what you hear from me you cannot utilize. Whatever you hear will spontaneously do what it likes.

Questioner: Sitting here and listening to Maharaj is pure joy. Even though it appears to be in duality, it strikes something deep inside.

M: So long as there is that sense of duality amongst you what you hear cannot reach the target.

Understand what I am saying. The consciousness arises spontaneously. Once I am conscious of myself I know I exist, and I love this beingness; I do not want this beingness to depart from me and it is this that makes me strive all the day till sleep overcomes me, in order to keep this love of beingness satisfied.

Then the Guru tells me the true state of affairs, that this consciousness which I love so much is only an illusion. It is the basic cause of all unhappiness and my true state is before this consciousness arose. That is beyond all concepts and any name given is a concept.

Understand it thoroughly, intuitively, beyond words, but also understand that that understanding can be of no use to you, because it is at the level of consciousness, and consciousness is illusory.

What is being recorded and transcribed here will be of unimaginable value in course of time when the basis of understanding will be broadened and people will want to know what the state of affairs is. At that time, when this is exposed on a wider scale, there will be wonderment. These words will be few, but those who at a certain time will be proud of their own achievements, when they hear these few words their own knowledge will evaporate so suddenly they will be wonderstruck.

Q: I don't understand the way the word consciousness is used here. I thought consciousness was pure awareness, the Ultimate reality.

M: This consciousness, which depends on the food body which is born, is time-bound. That which is prior to consciousness is the Absolute, and when consciousness is without a form and not aware of itself, it is the Absolute. We are nothing but this consciousness.

You come here and I talk to you but I am not concerned whether you come or go. I am totally independent. I, as the Absolute, do not need the consciousnes. Total independence is merely to apprehend and understand. My apparent dependence is on this consciousness which says "I Am." It is this sentience which enables me to perceive you. This concept I did not have but even then I existed. I was there before this consciousness appeared.

Whatever you want, desire or worship, can only be concepts. Have you heard what is conceptual existence and what is existence prior to concepts? Many people have come here purely for spiritual purposes and they have professed great love for me. Subsequently some good fortune happens to them and they prosper and in their prosperity they have no time to come here. All the earlier love is where? This is the province of *maya*. A person comes with the sincere intention of spiritual search, then this *maya* shows him a little bit of temptation and off he goes.

This *maya* does not operate independently — we are partners. Will he dare divorce himself from this *maya?* No, he will accept that *maya*. That ego (that I am so and so) is very difficult to get rid of, but the ego cannot touch one who really understands what I say.

You will continue coming here as long as the concepts remain; once you go beyond concepts there will be no need to come here.

Since when and because of what, is what you think you are?

December 23, 1980

Questioner: When you observe a problem, any problem in the human mind, if you observe it very strong and pure, the problem dissolves and there is only observation. What is that observation, who is that observation, what is the essence of that observation? How to go further?

Maharaj: This is a traditional way of understanding. It is a traditional mood of the world observation, nothing beyond that. Just a mood, that's all. When did this process of observing start? It started with the arrival of the waking state, deep sleep state, and the knowlege "I Am," all rolled into one "I Am." This is known as birth. With the so-called birth this triad has come, and with its arrival observation started. Every day it is going on. The moment the "I Amness" comes it is being used for experiencing, observing, etc.

Prior to the happening of this birth, where was that "I Amness"? It was not there.

Q: Going on further, one is in observation, one is just observing, is there any further question then? What should be the question?

M: When does the observation occur and of what? You have collected a profound vocabulary, but the Self-knowledge has not dawned.

Q: You see, that is what I was observing. How to enquire into that?

M: You know you are. Because you know you are, everything is happening. Get to know that knowledge "I Am." When you understand what that "I Amness" is, then the shell of the mystery is broken.

Q: What is the procedure to get at that?

M: You go to the source out of which this question arose. That source will solve this question.

Q: Is there any enquiry in that?

M: Oh yes. If anybody, any principle, wants to pose the question he should not embrace the body as himself. Pose the question from the standpoint that you are only the knowledge "I Am."

Q: You put the question because you don't know.

M: Yes, but the primary ignorance is about our "I Amness." We have taken it as the Ultimate, that is ignorance. We presume that this consciousness is the eternal, the Ultimate, that is the mistake. This "I Am" principle is there provided the waking state and deep sleep are there. I am not the waking state, I am not the deep sleep — therefore I, the Absolute, am not that "I Am." Leave aside this triad; what are you?

Q: It comes again to the question "Who am I?"

M: Understand clearly. When you keep aside the very instrument of questioning, where is the question?

Q: If you don't question. . . .

M: Which you? You have removed that "you."

Q: I don't know. How can you answer?

M: What questions can you have without this triad? Let us presume that you are fifty years old. You have had the association of that triad for fifty years; go behind now, five years earlier what was your experience? What were you like?

Q: I don't know.

M: That is correct. It was a no-knowing state. In that no-knowing state, suddenly knowingness has appeared. It has created all this mischief. Since when are you and how long will you continue to be?

Q: Well, I would say, since I have been experiencing and for as long as I am experiencing.

M: Right. Now, without the experience of "I Amness," talk something about that.

Q: I can't.

M: The association with this triad state, this bundle of mischief, due to what?

For example, a building is on fire, it is said because of a short circuit in the electricity. The arrival of this triad, due to what short circuiting? There was some friction.

When you press here on the cigarette lighter the flame is there; because of the friction or short circuiting, all the three states are aflame.

Q: And the flame is?

M: "I Am."

Q: I have been born into this.

M: Because of that triad you are experiencing life and doing spirituality also.

Q: At the end there is no question at all, no who am I or what am I if I put aside this triad there can only be silence.

M: Silence or peace is related to chaos or turbulence.

Q: It has nothing to do with peace and turbulence. I mean, if you just sit quiet in your Self, leaving aside these three states, knowing that I don't know myself, you can only be silent.

M: What you say is impossible. The knowingness will be there provided waking state and deep sleep are there. If they were not available you would not have been here in this form.

If you had the capacity to know before birth that you were being born, you would not have cared to jump into this pit of birth.

December 24, 1980

Maharaj: There is a great difference in my present state; earlier when I listened to *bhajans* I was conscious of the words and the deeper meaning of the words, and I was totally involved in the *bhajans*. Now my consciousness reacts only to the extent that there is consciousness of the *bhajans* taking place, but no involvement.

I am no longer concerned with anything to do with "me" or "mine." This sense of "me" and "mine" is so strong that there can be quarrels over nothing more than a little piece of cloth with no intrinsic value, simply because of the identification of "mine."

This consciousness is nothing but energy. When the body essence grows weaker, the consciousness grows weaker, and ultimately will leave; nothing is dead.

Food is one item that keeps this energy in good order. I take hardly any treatments, but I do have my body massaged. This massage revives the warmth in the body (which is the energy) so the energy in the body, which tends to be lax and cold, is warmed up again by the massage.

What is born is the waking and sleep states and the concept of time and consciousness. Once this consciousness is conscious of itself it takes on certain items as its own, because of conditioning, and others as not its own, and it will fight for and try to protect those which it considers its own. When consciousness realizes its potential power, its universality, the "me" and "mine" concept is lost.

This universal consciousness is known as God, which is the Almighty, the Omnipotent, Omniscient, and Omnipresent, all the attributes. These attributes are given to God in consciousness, not to the Absolute. The Absolute is without attributes.

December 27, 1980

Maharaj: The trouble is, everybody wants to have the knowledge of the Self without giving up the identification with the body, they are contradictory. Give up this identification and everything becomes simple. I am there before anything can happen. If anyone is asked whether he knows when the sky came into existence, he will say he does not know. He does not know because he considers his presence only as a phenomenon when the body was there.

That the sky was not there I know, and who is this? It is the One who is prior to everything. My true nature is not circumscribed by the concept of time and space.

When you hear this you promptly get confused and say, "In that case, how can I carry on my normal business?" Understand your true nature and then do any amount of business you like.

I say all this with great sincerity and great urgency. People hear it but do not give up the identification with the body. They hang on to it with great determination.

Even the statement that you existed before the sky existed will not be acceptable to you.

A child may be playing with the smallest coin, and if it is removed will be greatly agitated. You accept your identification with the same determination, the same anxiety, in spite of the knowledge which you are being given. Even if you give the child a toy made of gold, he will reject it because he has his heart set on that small coin. Even if I give you this knowledge, which is priceless, it will not be acceptable. The sound which first comes to denote the presence I am not; I am neither the presence nor the sound denoting the presence. Whatever one sees or perceives, that one must be prior to what is seen or perceived. It is simple.

When this knowledge of the Self gets firmer and firmer we are no longer attracted to those things which had previously attracted us so much. You see me talking, apparently at ease, but there is continual suffering, particularly between 2 and 4 p.m. the existence of this consciousness itself becomes unbearable. This is no one else's experience — I experience it myself.

What is being recorded now, when it is typed and put into book form and someone reads it, what will he make of it? He will say that he cannot imagine anyone having lived who could say this. The actual fact now is that I have reached a stage where it would require good fortune for anyone to have even a sight of that principle. The words are so profound, there is deeper meaning behind it. Presently only fortunate people will listen to my talks.

I repeatedly tell you that there is nothing save this consciousness, the knowledge "I Am" — if you feel like worshipping something, worship that. I am giving blessings. Blessings mean what? I am giving confidence and courage.

December 28, 1980

Maharaj: Can any of your concepts grasp the total, the Ultimate? Have you understood that knowledge itself is ignorance? If it were real it would have been there eternally — it would not have had a beginning and an end.

Now the experience "I Am" is felt, earlier that experience was not. When it was not, no proof was called for, but once it is, lots of proof is required.

How did you wake up in the morning? Why did you wake up at all? It is not the mind which knows — somebody knows because of the mind. Now my hand has lifted, who knows? The one who has lifted my hand knows it has lifted it. You are before the mind; because you are there the mind is working.

When will you wake up? Provided you are, you wake up.

Through the concepts of others you have built up so many things around you that you are lost. "You" is decorated and embellished by the concepts of others. Prior to receiving any hearsays from outside, has anyone any information about himself?

The purpose of *Sat-Guru* is to tell you what you are like prior to the building up of all those concepts of others. Your present spiritual storehouse is filled up with the words of others — demolish those concepts. *Sat-Guru* means the eternal state which will never be changed: what you are. You are that immutable, eternal, unchangeable Absolute. *Sat-Guru* tells you to get rid of all these walls built around you by the hearsays and concepts of others.

You have no form, no design. The names and forms you see are your consciousness only — the Self is colorless but it is able to judge colors, etc.

The one who is directed by a *Sat-Guru* has no more birth. Your *sadhana* is over, you have reached this place.

To you who search for the Self, I explain this type of knowledge, I lead you to a state where there is no hunger, no desire.

When you have knowledge you see the "I" as all-pervasive, as long as the consciousness is there, but the witness of the consciousness has no "I Am," that is your true eternal nature.

Giving up the body is a great festival for me.

December 29, 1980

Maharaj: Sitting in meditation helps the consciousness to blossom. It causes deeper understanding and spontaneous change in behavior. These changes are brought about in the consciousness itself, not in the pseudo-personality. Forced changes are at the level of the mind. Mental and intellectual changes are totally unnatural and different from the ones that take place in the birth principle. These take place naturally, automatically, by themselves, due to meditation.

Most of the people see the tree of knowledge and admire it, but what is to be understood is its source — the seed, the latent force from which it sprouts. Many people talk about it but only intellectually; I talk about it from direct knowledge.

A small speck of consciousness, which is like a seed, has all the worlds contained in it. The physical frame is necessary for it to manifest itself.

All the ambitions, hopes and desires are connected with an identity, and so long as there is an identity, no truth can be apperceived.

Questioner: Is there any destiny for the total manifestation or the phenomena as a whole?

M: As there is no single identity, where will it go? The fuel is the destiny of the flame; so also, the food essence body is the destiny of the consciousness. Consciousness alone offers destiny and destiny offers suffering. Because of the mistaken identity we think of personalized consciousness, but actually it is vast and limitless.

The source of consciousness is prior to time and space. Manifestation needs time and space, but the source of consciousness was there before manifestation took place. The manifestation has five elements, three *gunas* and, above all, consciousness, the "I Amness." Now how can anything be without my conscious presence? Even the elements cannot exist without me — I do not do anything, I do not create anything — they happen because of my conscious presence. My presence is throughout and I say this with conviction.

Some may read these words, some may have heard these words, some may hear the tape recordings, some may want to hear, but will be thrown so far away from the tapes, due to circumstances, that it won't be possible. There are millions of varieties of forms in the total manifestation, but the source of all is the consciousness. What is this consciousness? Does anyone think along these lines?

During a moment of complete attention to a questioner, the great strength of Mahahraj's character is revealed by the strong lines of his features in this striking photograph by Gordon Paterson.

The thoughtful and piercing eyes of Maharaj, which transfixed and inspired so many who came to sit before him, dominate his visage in this arresting photograph taken during a dialogue with suppliants.

Extending incense to prepare the altar surmounted by a picture of his own guru, Maharaj brings a sense of expectation and piety into the holy gathering as the prayer ritual begins.

In this small, humble room where Maharaj received devotees from all over the world, Jean Dunn (center), the editor of this volume, who was his long-time devotee and faithful recorder, joins other followers in devotions.

This attentive gathering of spiritual seekers, gathered to hear Maharaj impart wisdom and direction to their lives, includes Ramesh S. Balsekar (left foreground), considered to be Maharaj's most authentic interpreter and author of **Pointers from Nisargadatta Maharaj**; and Gordon Paterson, the sensitive photographer of Maharaj (right foreground).

In dreams one sees moons, stars, etc., but the identity is not there. The consciousness has to be understood during the waking state. People come and go, sights come and go, elements come and go, but I remain. I am conscious of my consciousness, and then alone the whole show is there.

Suppose a very important person is coming to visit in two months. The houses are decorated, the stands are put up, the streets are decorated, a lot of show is there. Why? It is due to that V.I.P.

Some people fast for a month, and take a lot of hardships on themselves, but they expect to get back more than they give away.

People look everywhere but to the source. Exclude this birth energy and see if anything can be done by anyone. We limit this limitless energy to the simple phenomenon which is one body. Intently examine the words: if my conscious presence is not there, what will I be? I enjoy the words that come up spontaneously and watch how true and unconditional they are.

A murderer is loose; he has committed many murders and the international police are after him but unable to catch him. That is like the traditional scriptures not being able to locate or find the Absolute. It is beyond the grasp of the *Vedas, Puranas,* etc., because it is not conceptual. This murderer is very proud to escape all the efforts of the police force; he is so fearless that he sits where the plans to catch him are discussed and hence he cannot be caught.

Everyone has to die, so die as your true nature. Why die as a body? Never forget your true nature. It may not be acceptable to many, but it is a fact. If you must have an ambition, have the highest, so that at least while dying, you will be the Absolute. Decide that now, firmly, with certainty and conviction.

A tiger is coming at you: you know that when he attacks you, death is certain. So, why die like a coward? Attack him and maybe he will run away. But if the tiger is passing by, do not unnecessarily attack him! Only when absolutely necessary, jump on him.

God is great and *maya* is vast, but what are you in the end? The mental modifications take you away from the Self. Nobody wants to enquire about the Self deeply and thoroughly; everybody enquires on a superficial level.

Q: My mind does not stay quiet, it goes here and there.

M: With all these ramblings you will be entertained, but you will not obtain knowledge. This is all spiritual entertainment, because the factual state of affairs is that what you are, you are, without modifications.

Q: The desires are there; they will keep on demanding.

M: Finally, what are you?

Q: I am nothing; mind, etc., keeps on going.

M: Then why are you learning all this?

Q: To serve the people.

M: So many great people have rendered so many great services, but where are they now?

Q: So many waves come and go. I want to pass my time by having no desires and serving others.

M: Do what you like. Rain falls and renders service to the beings. It does not suffer while rendering services. All the beings that come about are sustained due to rain, are they happy?

Q: They are all suffering. I too do not have peace. How does Maharaj see us?

M: I see everyone as I am. This being is the combination of the parents. All are engrossed in concepts, they enjoy them.

Q: When I am one with music, etc., it is all joy, but when I am in conflict, it is all misery. Sometimes I feel angry. Why?

M: Mind and body and their actions and reactions is not my subject. I do not deal with these problems. There are numerous other people who can deal with such problems.

Q: But almost all people are on the side of body-mind. One in one million is open to you.

M: Ask about yourself, do not bother about others.

Q: On one side I feel attracted towards silence and yet I feel that millions suffer and Sages do not do anything about them.

M: Because their suffering is illusory.

Q: I know that there are four states, waking, dreaming, deep sleep, and a state beyond all three. I can understand intellectually, but still suffering is there.

M: Get rid of all the four states and also rid the people of their suffering. Let the illusory world take care of itself, you must find out who you are.

Q: I want to practice Naturopathy and teach others and learn wisdom myself.

M: By developing these concepts you will not come out of it at all. First understand what is circumstantial and what is real. You are the product of the concepts of your parents, are you not?

Q: Yes, at a conceptual level.

M: Mind and all the concepts are due to your primary concept "I Am." Your parents and you are simultaneous concepts. Now, without trying to experience, what experience are you having?

Q: *I Am.*

M: Is it not a concept? There are concepts formed from concepts, it is a vast world of concepts.

Q: *I would like to be free from them.*

M: This is to be realized by one's self; it is not to be passed on by word of mouth. Who is obtaining the Self-knowledge directly? When did I happen to be? I must know about it myself, first-hand, not from others.

You are, you know you are — this is the great Lord, the sudden, explosive effulgence. Surrender to it, and you will know all. It is without form or name. It is to be abided in by firm conviction.

You could not see and judge the quality of light if you were not light yourself. You are that subtle knowledge, and if that is there, then only everything else is possible.

December 31, 1980

Questioner: *When you become one with everybody's consciousness there is an emotional drain because you feel their sorrow and everything. Is that a right state in which to be?*

Maharaj: It is one of the preliminary stages, but it is excellent. There is still separateness but gradually it will ripen into complete oneness.

Q: *I don't feel any desire anymore to strive for anything in the world.*

M: There is nothing wrong in that. Your hunger and thirst for bliss or joy is absolutely fulfilled and therefore you stop going after things.

Q: *Is there still some individuality left to continue one's duties?*

M: That individuality does not create any kind of discontent or fear. It so happens that there is no memory at all of that individual "I," it goes on acting on its own energy. There is a memory that this is the total manifestation but no memory of an individual acting.

Q: *I feel that I am one with consciousness but it wavers.*

M: You are not yet stabilized in consciousness; you are getting some glimpses. Being one with consciousness is going beyond these states of waking and sleeping. You know the sky, you know the space, but can you become one with the space? Not yet, it is not possible. When you become one with consciousness you become one with space.

Q: Is there something which I can do to help me to grow, to progress?

M: Consciousness does not undergo any progress. Even the space cannot have any progress and the space is number three.

One is the Absolute, two is consciousness, three is space. Where there was no knowledge "I Am," that is number one; later on there is the sense "I Am," that is number two; then there is space — number three. Passing the examination of the *Upanishads,* does it give you knowledge of the Self?

Q: No. However it does something.

M: In my case, everything is spontaneous — that is my *dharma*. If the knowledgeable people come and tell me I am foolish, I will say, "This foolishness is my richness, my freedom. That knowingness which has come over me, that itself is foolishness."

You are a very gentle woman; if someone comes and abuses you, thinking you are a man, you will get very angry at this misunderstanding. To identify with anything, "I am like this," is abuse of your nature.

Q: How to lose this identification with the body?

M: Increase the conviction that you are the formless consciousness. You develop your firm conviction that you are the total manifestation, universal consciousness. There is nobody who can have the knowledge of the Truth, the Eternal. It is one's eternal true state, but it is not a knowledgeable state — you cannot know It. So-called knowledge is boundless and plenty in the state of attributes, "I Am."

In this body is the knowledge "I Am." When the body drops down the knowledge "I Am" will subside there only — what remains is the Absolute.

January 1, 1981

Questioner: Does the universe exist without me?

Maharaj: When you did not have the consciousness were you concerned with the world? The world will exist as long as consciousness is there.

Don't get involved in too many questions and answers. Do meditation, so that the knowledge becomes one with the knowledge. Then all the answers will spring up spontaneously. I have given you the key. Mine is the state where there are no fears, no desires, no ambitions.

Q: By meditation, will I reach that state?

M: You must meditate, but there is nothing to reach — you *are* that state.

Q: When you are very active in the world it is very easy to identify with the body.

M: It is not because of the activities that you identify with the body, it is because of the identification with the body that the activities are claimed.

Q: It is easier not to be identified if you are not involved in activities.

M: That is a concept. In you there cannot be any change; it is your presumption that there will be some change in you. You are talking to me from the standpoint of body identification.

You are trying to obtain something — a spiritual object. Forget that. Merely see what that is with which you identify yourself, the body. Find out the source of the body. When you understand that, there will be no need of any spiritual search.

Q: There is no opportunity to find out because you have to do your work.

M: The two are not connected. You can find this out even in the thick of battle. How did this body arise, what is the source?

If you are asked to give up this or that in your daily activities, that is not true. Forget about giving up anything — do all your normal business as best you can, but all that can go on only so long as the consciousness is there. Keep in mind only not to hurt others.

Do's and don'ts are given so that the affairs in the world may go on smoothly.

Whatever you have been told or have read will take you nowhere. Find out first, what is it because of which I know I exist — that is the consciousness. The entire universe is based on the concept "I Am." It is illusory, imaginary, there is no substance to it.

January 2, 1981

Questioner: It seems that I am more and more busy, and I don't have much time anymore for meditation. I want instruction from Maharaj on how to come to Self-realization.

Maharaj: Carry on your work in the world but your work can only take place if you are there — the sense of being must be there. That is enough.

Q: Is it necessary for me to constantly remind myself of that, to be aware of that?

M: Who can be conscious of consciousness other than consciousness itself? Is there any other entity? It is there, the consciousness is always aware of itself. The trouble is that consciousness has identified with the body. Do nothing else except this: do not identify the consciousness with a body.

By doing something or not doing something, is there any change in the consciousness? There is no need of any *sadhana* except being aware of the fact that it is only in this consciousness that everything takes place.

Relatively you are the consciousness and the consciousness has no form. You can only *sense* consciousness, you cannot *see* it. You know it; you know that you are.

Who directs the body to do what it does? It can only be the consciousness, there is no entity. Consciousness does whatever is to be done through the various bodies. You are that consciousness and the love that consciousness has for itself.

Q: Then there is really nothing in particular that you can do to realize this and you can't try to do nothing. It just is. That's the way it is and that's all.

M: Yes. Just understand. Just be your Self.

Q: Should one have faith in the Self?

M: Once you are your Self, where is the question of faith? Just be your Self. Operation is brought to a standstill. When you are that, it is finished — the circle is closed, you are your Self.

That Self-realization is God, the Self itself is God. Religion teaches that a God is made in the form of a body because people identify themselves with a body; the image of God is also made in the form of a body. What I am teaching you is that you are the God; to abide in the Self is Godly. Presently you understand a Krishna, Christ, Buddha, or a prophet as a God, but as a personality they are not Gods. God means the consciousness "I Am" — it has no form, no name. Because Christ, or Buddha, or Krishna realized themselves, their consciousness, they became Godly. For the people to understand, they are indicated as Gods, but God cannot be named, cannot be conditioned into a body. To abide in the Self, stabilize in the Self, that is God. My Guru delivered me into Godliness.

Q: Despite the apparent suffering a person may have, is there ever a time when what Maharaj says is not true, not a fact? I mean, you are always the Self, whether or not you are aware of it.

M: A little higher now. Consciousness is there, but it is not merely consciousness but some principle which knows the consciousness. That principle, together with the consciousness, is there.

Christ did exist as a person some 2,000 years back; prior to that, did you exist or not?

Q: I must have.

M: You did exist prior to Christ also — that you have to understand. The one that witnesses the consciousness knows that the consciousness was not there.

Q: That witnessing of the consciousness, that's not like the normal kind of experience we have, right?

M: If experiencing is there it is because of the appearance of the consciousness. If the consciousness is not there, no experience.

Q: But Maharaj is saying that there is something prior to consciousness which can be experienced.

M: No. It is not experienced. That principle knows or witnesses consciousness; if the consciousness is not there, the witnessing stops. You cannot conceptually know it, you alone have to become That.

The Ultimate principle is there. Consciousness in the form of a Christ, or a Krishna came, the personalities were there, and those were identified as Gods because they stabilized in their consciousness. Due to that Ultimate principle only, consciousness has appeared. When this consciousness was not there, where was Christ or where was Krishna? They were the Absolute only.

Before manifestation can take place there must be something which has manifested itself: that is the Absolute.

Q: I can understand that what Maharaj says has to be the case, but how does he know that?

M: That you are and the world exists, how did you know? Did anybody have to tell you? If you were the only man on earth you would still know that.

Q: I just know it.

M: Spontaneously you know; everything is like that. There can never be an understanding of this as long as you are thinking in terms of an entity, intellectually. Really, the truth is like a speck, everything is contained in that speck of consciousness.

I know what the position was before Christ or Buddha, etc., acquired the body. Whatever the form and the consciousness within, it is time-bound. I am timeless.

Q: Jesus said, "Before Abraham was I am." Abraham was the father of the Jewish race.

M: Ah-h-h, that's it! That I know.

January 5, 1981

Questioner: Although the individual body has a limited time span, consciousness is, in another sense, unlimited, as the bodies are infinite in number and always changing; correct?

Maharaj: That is correct. Consciousness is the material of creation.

Q: When one is completely submerged in consciousness, to an extent that there is no separate entity, does it follow that everything, the past, future, the present, is present in that, that there is really no such thing as time?

M: That is correct.

Q: Everything that exists is consciousness, and is in consciousness only, and although the human body is different from a flower, isn't it true that they are both only consciousness? The difference is in appearance only, but exactly the same in substance?

M: Everything is different in appearance. What is the same is the all-pervading consciousness. What is difficult to understand? The five elements, everything one sees, is made up of these.

Q: Is it correct to say that consciousness unmanifested is the Absolute, and the Absolute manifested is consciousness?

M: By having intellectual acrobatics one cannot realize the Ultimate. You are trying to circumscribe what is unlimited into that which is limited, the intellect.

I am almost illiterate; why do people come here to see me? What is the intellectual status of this lady? She is a Ph.D. Why does she come here? When I see you what am I looking at? Look at the birth principle, that dot, the point which was born. You are a product of the objective material, that drop. Did somebody create this body?

Q: No, it just came out of that drop.

M: Then why are you categorizing all these happenings? Just focus your attention on this point. Whatever you are presently is the product of that birth drop. Focus your attention on that and everything will be revealed to you. If you, as an entity, want to make an intellectual study of this subject, don't come to see me. Here it is you only; get in the test tube.

Why do you get entangled in the branches and leaves; why don't you go to the seed? Without the seed the tree would not be there. Find out where the seed comes from. This is what I am taking you back to again and again. Whatever I have to suffer, physical or otherwise, is due to what? It begins with self-love, the need to be present. This consciousness is the cause of all suffering. This love of being, love of self, love of consciousness, is the nature of what? It is the nature of the seed, the sperm. The consciousness was latent in that to which the name birth is given. Where is the one who understands this?

Having got the spiritual knowledge, why do you want to reduce it to pen and paper?

People will hear what I say, but hardly anyone will put it into practice. I did not have a long association with my Guru. My Guru merely told me, "You are not this, you are This." That is all. I accepted it with such conviction that the knowledge has flowered into what has come.

Out of food essence, the taste "I Am." The Absolute has no taste, no color, no design. You cannot be witnessed by you; only what is other than you can be witnessed by you.

January 6, 1981

Questioner: After death can I help other people to reach the light?

Maharaj: After death you will not remember that you are. You must know what death is. You are talking about existence after this life; do you remember any past lives?

Q: I was on an island, helping other people in my last life.

M: Do you remember your parents?

Q: No.

M: What is the proof that you were born there?

Q: I don't know.

M: This is only imagination, a phantasy, a concept occurring to you. If, at the time of death the consciousness entertains a very strong concept, the consciousness can create that particular concept. Suppose that at the

time of death the person imagines having a life somewhere — the consciousness will create a similar situation. The realm of consciousness is
not eternal. The consciousness is a fraud. All of these things are illusions
in the realm of consciousness.

Q: Consciousness is always manifested, isn't it?

M: Consciousness will be there as long as a particle of space will be
available.

Q: Is it helpful to go into seclusion to realize that?

M: Yes.

Q: To go out of the ordinary life?

M: Not like that. You need not go out of your family life.

Q: What kind of seclusion?

M: Even among this crowd be alone, abide in your own Self. Focus
your attention on your Self.

Q: Does it matter if one does not understand intellectually but simply has devotion?

M: If you have that devotion, knowledge will proliferate out of it. When
it is said that out of devotion somebody meets a God, it is not a personality God, but the devotee himself proliferates into the knowledge,
into profundity — he becomes Godly. That God will be so long as the
devotee knows himself; when the devotee subsides into nothingness, the
God also subsides into nothingness. You have to come to the conclusion
that in the final analysis your balance sheet is nil.

Out of the essence of the digested food in the body the "I Amness" is
there. What you are presently is the outcome of this food material. If the
food isn't available, where are you? What about all this profound knowledge which you have collected?

Don't arrogate to yourself the doership of anything — it is all happening. If you are not, what is the need for all the disciplines, including
God? Even if you are fully convinced about this, you are reduced to
nothing; nevertheless, on the death bed you will take the last drop of
medicine to survive.

This is real liberation: to know that you are nothing. All your knowledge, including yourself, is liquidated — then you are liberated.

If you think that you have done some great deed, then you will be
planning to go to heaven, you are obsessed by concepts, you are not
liberated. This knowledge is fit for that one who has devotion to the
Guru; only that person is fit to receive this knowledge.

Q: Although we have been listening to these talks for many years, we never feel exhausted.

M: There is that fascination to listen to this again and again. You are not collecting words and storing them, you are getting the impact of the words and then letting them go.

January 10, 1981

Questioner: Does consciousness work through the mind?

Maharaj: Everything takes place in consciousness. I have long ago given up my independent identity, there is no question of an independent entity, everything is an appearance in consciousness only.

As in any piece of cloth the main element is the thread, so in any appearance the essence is the consciousness. This must be deeply apperceived and this cannot happen as long as there is identification with the body. As long as identification is there you will think of benefiting only this pseudo-personality.

The whole universe is alive as long as you have this consciousness, once gone from you, nothing is there. Understand, there is a difference between someone who speaks from book learning and someone who speaks from experience.

A *jnani* identifies with the universal consciousness and so there is a perfect adaptation to everything and every place. Only witnessing is taking place. This psychosomatic apparatus is there both for the *jnani* and the ignorant, but the ignorant one who identifies with the body, is happy or unhappy, as the situation changes. The *jnani* only witnesses, he is not individually concerned with what happens.

I repeat again and again, please listen; understand what it is because of which we feel alive, understand the nature of it, understand the taste of it, then the body identification will go.

This *Atman Prem* (Self love), this beingness, has come about with no effort on your part. What is its nature, its taste, what is it? That you must find out.

Fix your identity firmly in this beingness, do not give it limbs, shape or form, for once you give it form you have limited it.

Understand this energy which is behind the entire manifestation of the universe.

You ask many questions, you look for the answers in books and words, not in intuitive experience. This is not knowledge. Knowledge springs from the consciousness without effort, of its own accord.

Various names have been given to this energy which is the source of all manifestation. People pray to these names and forms, they do not pray to that beingness, that substance, which these names represent. Pray to that beingness only.

As there is no separateness between two genuine friends, as a genuine friend knows the needs of the other without speaking, who cares for him and does it spontaneously, so you should develop such a deep friendship with that substance, not in the attitude of praying for favors, but as a friend seeking a friend. Be one with the knowledge "I Am," the source of sentience, the beingness itself.

People think and talk about everything else except this basic thing which I have told them. They are interested in scientific miracles, they make science a God, they concern themselves with these shapes which are already manifest. They are not interested in the original miracle, this body and its life force.

We ignore this miracle. If there is no consciousness there is no God. The existence and essence of God are both in this consciousness, and therefore in this body.

How did these temples and churches come about? Because of the inspiration of the consciousness within the body. The consciousness is the seed of Brahman, God, of everything, events only happen and manifest when consciousness is there, and in the body is the consciousness.

Nothing I say will benefit you in this world, I only tell you what you are. If you are seeking that kind of peace which is priceless, it can only be in establishing yourself in the consciousness with steadfast conviction. By conviction I mean never doubted, firm, unshakeable, never wavering — have that kind of conviction in your beingness. Think of nothing else, pray to nothing else. *Atman Prem,* because of it everything is.

At the moment of what is called death, what happens? All it means is that a speck of consciousness is given up. This speck is given up to a concept you have accepted as time, you reluctantly hand it over to time. The *jnani* gives it up to his own true nature.

This *Atman Prem,* this existence which we have protected for so many years, to whom shall we give it up? If ignorant, to our concept of time. If ignorant *bhakti* (devotee), to a concept of God. If *jnani,* to his own true nature.

Whatever you think you have got as an identity, have you acquired it by effort or intention? Is there anything you have really got? No. This body, this consciousness, has come spontaneously, so sleep comes when it likes, even waking and sleep are not in your control. What is yours? Who has this knowledge of the Self by his own effort?

This pseudo entity thinks that it is he who is active and doing. I am talking to you now as consciousness. Can any one of you give me an indication of that knowledge, that beingness that you are?

Q: Consciousness thanks consciousness over and over again.

M: That about which nothing can be said, I have said. Accept that drop, taste it and swallow it.

Hear this: God can only exist in the heart of man, not elsewhere. You identify with the body and limit yourself, and yet, remember, do not neglect this body, this is the house of God, take care of it. Only in this body can God be realized.

It is only for an analytic understanding that God, your body, your Self, have been divided, but it is one Self, each is intimately related.

January 19, 1981

Maharaj: This sense of presence, is it not the most acceptable thing, as far as you are concerned — do you not love it the most?

Why are you sitting here? You are sitting here for yourself, because you want something for yourself. What is it that you are? Go into that. You have no doubt that you are present, so what is it that makes you want to continue all the time?

Aeons of time have come and gone. During this time millions of forms have been created and destroyed. Do they have a sense of being present? Are they worried about themselves? There is nothing you can do without this sense of presence and there is nothing you can do to continue it.

Questioner: Why does it love to continue?

M: That is its nature. Consciousness and love are the same thing. Ask yourself, what is it that you want, what are you after? You consider yourself an entity and want something. If consciousness were not there would you need anything?

What you hear is totally different from what you expected to hear.

Q: Am I to identify myself with consciousness?

M: What is this "you" other than consciousness? Are they two? There is no entity who can do anything in the world; there is no entity who can do any spiritual search. If there is no entity there is no bondage and no liberation. Just understand this: there is nothing to be done. Whatever I am telling you, hear it and discard it. Before you acquired this body and had this sense of presence, tell me what had you done? After this sense of presence, the knowledge "I Am," then you have been shown a sort of TV film: "This is your family, these are your parents." Do you personally have any experience of any of this?

Understand what has been created and will be destroyed; understand what you are that cannot suffer anything.

I have come to the conclusion that consciousness and whatever appears in consciousness is nothing but a gigantic fraud. There is no one who has committed this fraud — it is a spontaneous happening. There is no perpetrator of this fraud.

This speck of consciousness creates Gods of mud and earth which, having been accepted, give us whatever we pray for. Having understood this fraud, also understand that there is nothing that can be done about it, therefore all that can happen is for the understanding to take place.

This body and the taste of the body — that is the understanding. Is not the body the essence of food and is not consciousness the nature of the essence of food? There is a very simple question one must keep in mind; what authority or control do I have over my own existence? Therefore what can one do by one's own efforts?

Understand that the total manifestation is the child of a barren woman, but, having understood it, give full attention to your work and let that work be done as efficiently as possible. Take good care of this work that you do in the world because it is an orphan.

January 20, 1981

Maharaj: The Absolute is . . . to give you an idea, there is a place in India where you have never been; if a description were given it would still remain a description for you. The universal consciousness, the beingness, is anything that is seen. When the universal consciousness manifests itself as a phenomenon, the phenomenon is that limited form which thinks that it is independent but is not. The phenomenon is the manifestation of consciousness; when it is not manifested it is immanent in everything. If you think you have understood, it is not so. Anything that you know is not the truth.

The body is made up of the five elements and each body behaves according to the proportion of the combination of the five elements. So long as one is identified with the essence of the five elements it is impossible to understand, because that which is trying to understand is a pseudo entity. The biggest drawback to understanding is the concept that I am an entity and, secondly, that any concept I have is the truth.

It is only when it is understood with the greatest conviction that there is no entity, and what is happening is merely the program of the functioning of consciousness — there is merely the functioning, there is no entity who is causing it and there is no entity who is suffering — only then can the disidentification take place. Otherwise all kinds of misconceptions occur.

You have not understood until you have solved the riddle of the one who thinks he has understood.

Do I identify myself with the dirt which I blow from my nose? The stuff of which this body has been created, is it any different?

I am neither the material from which the body has been created nor the consciousness which is immanent in that material.

January 27, 1981

Maharaj: Where are you from and who directed you here?

Questioner: I have been studying in a monastery in Thailand and the Abbot suggested I read the books of Maharaj's teachings. When I decided to come to India several friends, who had been to see Maharaj, told me to come here.

M: Do you have questions?

Q: Will Maharaj explain what is the method of practice he recommends?

M: There is no practice or discipline to be followed. Merely listen to me and accept what I tell you with firm conviction.

Q: What about the importance of meditation?

M: The only thing which anyone has is the conviction that one exists, the conscious presence. Meditation is only on that sense of presence, nothing else.

Q: During the meditation period one just sits and thinks of one's presence.

M: Not as an individual sitting, but the sense of presence without words. Meditate on that which knows you are sitting here. Your feeling that your body is here is identification with the body, but that which knows that this body is sitting here is the expression of the Absolute.

Q: Is this known with the mind?

M: Mind is the nature of the material; you are not the material, you are that which understands the material. That sense of presence will explain anything that is necessary for you to understand. Your effort will not do it, but that sense of presence, with which you become one, will do it.

Q: Should I develop this sense of presence throughout the day, in all my activities?

M: It is not necessary for you to concentrate on it, it is always there. Whatever you do, the essence of it is the body-mind. Let the body-mind do its work but understand that what is doing the work is not you, you are the sense of presence.

Whatever efforts you make, either physically or intellectually, will be essentially the effort of the body-mind. There is nothing for you to do. Whatever happens will happen by itself, with your conviction that you are totally apart from body and mind.

Q: That sounds easy, but it must be very hard.

M: Whatever you think, easy or hard, you stick to one conviction, that you are that sense of presence and not the body-mind. That which you are has no shape or color.

Q: Does that sense of presence continue after the body and mind go?

M: When the body goes that sense of presence will go and consciousness will no longer be conscious of itself.

Q: When the body goes, everything goes?

M: Correct. There is no experience of either happiness or unhappiness, there is no need of experience either.

Q: Is there nothing that continues — nothing?

M: You are thinking at a conceptual level. At that level, who is there who wants to know? Forget about That state.

Q: I would like to understand That.

M: Whatever can be understood or perceived can never be the eternal Truth. The Unknown is the Truth.

I have no need of any experience, therefore I have no need to quarrel with anybody. The body and mind will go on doing whatever they like during their natural course of duration.

Q: Is it better to do one thing than another? For instance, with this mind and body I could just sit and do nothing, or I could go around helping people, doing good things. Which would be better to do?

M: The body and mind will do whatever is natural for that combination.

Q: You can control things — for example you can eat too much or drink too much, things like that — or else you can do good things, helping people, etc.

M: These are the do's and don'ts regarding the body-mind, which you are not; that is the premise from where you have started. Understand that when there is no body, consciousness is not conscious of itself. So long as the body is there, the body must do its natural functioning.

Q: Then I just let it do what's natural?

M: There is no question of your allowing it to happen, it *will* happen, you have no control over it.

Q: But some things I can control. If I come here or I stay outside — I can control that.

M: That is a misconception. Whatever happens, happens by itself. All this is the show, or the expression, of consciousness — the nature of it is change. It is the dance of the conscious presence. There are so many ways in which consciousness entertains itself, many different forms, abilities, capacities are functioning, but the functioning is merely to entertain itself. When it is tired, it rests in sleep, when awake it needs some kind of entertainment, some movement, some doing.

They are all appearances in consciousness; each will last according to its own duration, but basically, nothing that happens has any validity or importance. Until the awakening, or understanding, you think that you are the doer, but once this apperception takes place you know there is no entity that is working.

Q: I just think it would be best to do good things instead of bad things.

M: What do you mean by good and bad things? Good things in one set of circumstances can be bad things in another set of circumstances. Even the things you consider good can be so only as long as the body lasts. Only a rare one will realize there is nothing to do — he is already That.

Q: Maharaj is helping us, is that a volitional state?

M: It is part of the total functioning. What is taking place is sort of a dream state and whatever happens will be part of the dream. Whatever happens out of me, either spiritual or worldly, will not multiply into mind modifications, because any actions are universal and spiritual. The spirituality is perfect because of stabilization in the Unknown.

Many times the witnessing of physical pain happens to me, because the body and the consciousness are still there, an instrument to register pleasure and pain; because of my health the pain is registered more. I was witnessing that pain earlier, but since you have come it is gone. When you are established in consciousness it is full of joy only. I was established in that consciousness and full of joy, but suddenly the disease has appeared and the pain has come. So long as you are established in consciousness and do not have any physical disorder, you will not have any experience of pain. That is the quality of that consciousness itself.

You are prior to the consciousness. In that state there is no pleasure or pain.

The association of the body and consciousness is something like this: you are a bachelor and you are having a happy free life; with the association with a wife, the pleasure and pain results begin. It is just like that.

Q: How can I acquire that state?

M: It always prevails but It is beyond knowing. That state cannot be elucidated, these are merely pointers, "There It is" — words cannot enter that state.

February 1, 1981

Questioner: Maharaj says that the world exists only when the consciousness arises in me. Does it mean that the world exists only so long as the consciousness exists, as far as I am concerned?

Maharaj: The world exists so long as this sense of presence is there. The sense of presence is in consciousness — not my consciousness or your consciousness but universal consciousness. The total manifestation of the universe depends upon this sense of presence, the general sense of presence. When this sense of presence disappears, where is your universe?

Other than the three states: waking, sleep and "I Amness," I have no experience, but neither can I give up these three states. I am loaded with them, I cannot get rid of them. They have come without my knowledge. Nobody asked me if I wanted these three states.

I do not consider any of you to be different from me; at the same time, as far as I am concerned, I have wiped out the total existence and therefore, since there is no individuality, there are no bindings on the words that come out of me. With the giving up of individuality, all the poses go — that one is a *sannyasi,* a *jnani,* or something else. Along with a pose are restrictions, "I am so and so, I must not say such and such." The whole thing is an illusion, merely entertainment.

Consider from your own experience, is there anything constant? Even your own image of yourself is always changing.

My own experience is that nothing has really happened in this world. The seeker, the seeking and the sought — none of these three is true. Nothing is happening — everything that goes on in the world is a fraud. When will you come to an understanding or to peace? Only when you understand this fact and understand the spiritual truth, only then will peace descend.

Q: What is the ultimate truth?

M: You. You can get as frustrated and angry as you like, it does not disturb me at all. My state is unchanging.

Q: Are my experiences in meditation the truth?

M: All experiences are in time, time-bound. Truth is not time-bound.

February 2, 1981

Questioner: How can I make the surrender to the Guru permanent?

Maharaj: Have you not been told that there is nothing permanent in this world? That is the search itself — what am I when this temporary state is gone and before it came?

You have a clock which is made to last for 100 years. At the end of that 100 years the clock stops — it has served its purpose. When the clock of the body stops, the same thing has happened — that body has served the purpose of consciousness.

Q: Total surrender means two, something joining, one surrendering to another.

M: During that temporary state in consciousness, everything is correct. Whatever the plot of the story, it is correct, but the story is fiction.

What I am telling you is absolutely open — an open secret. There is nothing that I keep hidden from you. Try and understand. It is merely a question of understanding.

Q: Guru's grace is always there.

M: Guru is not an individual. You are thinking in terms of a form. The consciousness is all pervading. You find out what is this "you" that is seeking grace. In that body the "I Am" is ticking — that is the Guru. You worship that "I Am" principle and surrender to that Guru and that Guru will give you all the grace.

In consciousness there can exist nothing without its interrelated counterpart. The moment you say knowledge, knowledge can only be in ignorance, so this knowledge one has about Guru is also ignorance. When will the knowledge be Guru? When that knowledge and the ignorance both disappear into *vijnana*. *Jnana* is knowledge, *ajnana* is ignorance, both disappear into *vijnana*.

Q: *I am caught in that process of watching the body-mind.*

M: Dream occurs in objective, material, manifestation, in the consciousness. It is not you, it is something other — objective, material. What you call "I Am" and birth, you are not that, it is material. Suppose that there is a Muslim boy that I have adopted; I have not sired that boy, but I now claim him as "my" boy. Like that, this "I Amness" is not directly me, it is something other, something material, something Muslim, I am not that. I, the Absolute, have nothing to do with that.

People are sometimes confused because they expect an answer which is based on their concepts. You ask someone to bring you a spoon, and instead he brings you a needle. Both are words, both are knowledge, but that is not what you want. What you will receive is the true knowledge, even if what you are asking for is not the true knowledge.

Q: *I must reach that level to be able to understand.*

M: There are millions of grains, made into millions of forms, but the seed is only one. All these millions of forms are because of some particular seed, but I am not that seed.

The Ultimate knowledge does not have any knowledge. This knowledge "I Am" has appeared spontaneously, as a result of the body. See it as it is, understand it as it is.

When the waking state is gone, sleep begins, when sleep is gone, the waking state begins. When both are gone, I am at home. Why did they leave me? Because it was all foreign, it was not me.

Take this advice: better not to be trapped in the spiritual knowledge business; have a nice time, a good life, be of service to others, and in due course, when the time is ripe, you will die.

Q: *Without your advice, millions of people are already following your advice.*

February 3, 1981

Maharaj: The knowledge that I am expounding will dissolve your identity as a personality and will transform you into manifest knowledge. The manifest knowledge, the consciousness, is free and unconditioned. It is not possible to either catch hold of or give up that knowledge because you *are* that knowledge, subtler than space.

This knowledge that you are the manifest must be opened through meditation; you do not get it by listening to words.

Is not this consciousness prior to any other experience and is there not something on which this consciousness has come about? That waking state, deep sleep and the sense of presence, who has these experiences other than That which was prior to these experiences?

That which is talking to you is that state which is time-bound, which has come temporarily upon my original state. Therefore you and I can have no sense of fear; it is only this changing state which has identified with the body which has fear.

The fear of death is the fine for accepting the identity of the body as a separate entity in the total functioning. It is only birth which fears death.

Presence and absence are interrelated dualities, this was understood only after the sense of presence arose, earlier there was no sense of either absence or presence.

Questioner: *What if we understand only intellectually and we have not yet realized?*

M: The big advantage of even intellectually understanding is that you will not be bound by fear of death. Birth did not give you anything and death can take nothing from you.

According to the world I have this terrible disease; I keep on talking exactly as I talked earlier, it has no effect on me. Only that which has taken birth will disappear, how am I affected?

You are fortunate to hear what I say. Listen, but do not make any effort to understand it, because only your intellect can try to understand and intellect does not reach That. What you have heard will have its own results; do not interfere.

Even if you have certain emotions of fear, etc., understand that they are of that chemical of which the body and mind are made. You have nothing to do with that temporary state.

In the name of spirituality many people commit a lot of atrocities on the body, thinking they will get superior knowledge. From where and what? What are they going to gain?

This knowledge is — provided I am.

February 17, 1981

Maharaj: I am neither a Guru nor a disciple. This is all the play of the five elements. Body is just a biological development, a vegetation growth, and we take pride in it, asserting that *I am* somebody. But this is just a natural growth, just like plants.

Questioner: Is the experiencer eternal?

M: If the experiencer had been eternal he would have not made enquiries, asking what is this, what is that. Had he been eternal he would already have had all the knowledge of this objective world.

Q: How can we find the way that is meant for us?

M: If your urge to realize the Self is very intense, your urge and the consciousness will direct you in the correct course.

Q: Sometimes when I understand, something happens to me. I either get tense or I begin shaking in my head or neck and sometimes there are noises going on in my head. I don't understand it. Should I ignore it or what?

M: Just ignore it. Those are good signs.

Q: Physical sickness is there sometimes.

M: It is not sickness, it is the expression of the five elemental body.

Q: Can one realize through nama-mantra?

M: So many sages have developed into the highest state only through *nama-mantra.* Whatever you recite should merge into you, prior to mind.

Q: Some people tell about Gurus giving power and energy.

M: It is possible. I have deliberated only on my Self.

Q: Trances, visions, samadhi — *did Maharaj go through all those experiences?*

M: Any number of them. I did not take delivery of all those experiences.

Q: Why do some people go through it and others don't?

M: The design of each seeker is different. According to the seeker's quality, he will encounter experiences. There have been so many Self-realized Sages, but each one's experience has been different because the qualities have been different. The experiences of Rama and Krishna were different. Any *jnani* discards the experiences; he does not get associated with them. He does not hang on to them or try to invoke them again.

February 18, 1981

Questioner: This identity with a body, as an entity, is present. Could anyone, at any stage, have done anything which could have prevented this identification?

Maharaj: It is the nature of this beingness to associate itself with a form. How can an imagined entity separate itself?

Q: Is this wanting to be separate also natural, a part of nature?

M: Yes. It is all part of natural functioning — part of the show. The entire thing is a concept. All that can be done is to understand.

Look at the apparent contradiction: my own form is suffering, when that is known more people come here, more people receive advantages. Those advantages happen automatically, spontaneously — I am not working for those advantages which you get.

The talking which I do, and your listening, is part of the total functioning. You consider it as one individual listening to another individual, that is not so. What you hear is universal consciousness. This knowledge is not to be conveyed to a human being who is a spiritual infant. The human being is trying to collect benefits for an individual. When this identification is given up, the receptivity for the talks will be created. From an enormous tank of water you dip a tiny tumbler full and say, "This is me."

Whatever status and achievements one has attained will remain only so long as the name and form remain; once they have gone where is the entity who thinks he has achieved something? If this is deeply apperceived how can anything in the world bother you?

What I am talking about is this original concept, the consciousness, before which there was nothing. Whatever is in this original concept will remain only so long as the consciousness is there — then we go back to our original nature. When consciousness exposes itself to you and shows you your true nature, then you will have no form. Without a form can there be an image?

The entire manifestation is a hallucination, the nature of which is to be inconstant.

February 22, 1981

Questioner: What should I do during the day? What kinds of thoughts or actions should I have in order to find out my true nature and have peace of mind?

Maharaj: Any thoughts or actions will be based on body-mind identity and in order to see your true nature there must be abandonment of this identity with the phenomenal center. This cannot come by any volitional action — it happens without any special efforts. There is no question of *doing* anything because there is no one to do anything.

The mind can only work with some name or form or image. If you give this up, the mind will be helpless. What I am saying about your true nature is so simple that the mind cannot grasp it.

What is has always been there. Give up conceptualizing and what *is* remains. People will stop only at seeing the manifest. Who will go *behind* the manifest and see that the manifest and unmanifest are not two — they are one?

The manifest is seen as light, the unmanifest as dark, but what *is* is the same thing — That which perceives both.

For the one who has abandoned the identification it is simple. Words can only point at something. That which *is* is neither like me or like you, it is not even aware of what it is. Only when consciousness is conscious of itself can there be knowledge of anything. It is prior to any knowledge. It is very simple. People who are considered to be very learned come here, how do I see them? I see them as being in total ignorance.

Q: Why is there a fear of darkness?

M: Your question is totally irrelevant. Go to the source without which neither light or darkness could be cognized. What is the use of talking about what is objective when I have told you to go to the subject?

Q: I consider myself to be good or bad at different times.

M: This can only be with identification with the body; abandon this. From now on I will only say what the position is, thereafter you must perceive. I have no physical resources for a dialogue. Whatever you hear cannot and will not go to waste.

February 23, 1981

Maharaj: If you have really understood the core of the matter no questions can arise. Questions arise only to an entity. The question is usually — "What can I do?". Where the "I" itself is not, who will want to know anything? Every manifestation is an appearance in consciousness, perceived and cognized by consciousness. There is only manifestation functioning and perceiving.

Questioner: My mind is too agitated for consciousness to be in consciousness.

M: You have not been listening carefully to what I have said. The words have not reached you. I have told you that consciousness is always there and anything that happens is in consciousness, so let consciousness remain in consciousness.

Why do you, considering yourself as a separate entity, try to meddle in it? All that *is* is consciousness.

Q: Can I ask about the meaning of suffering?

M: Now you are developing a new concept — that there is something meaningful or profound behind suffering. This concept itself is going to strangulate you. Any concept erupting out of you — how can it give you knowledge? You must get rid of all concepts. You are the very basis, the foundation, out of which concepts erupt. You are not the concepts, you are prior to concepts. You must be firmly convinced about this.

Q: Do I suppress the concepts?

M: Leave them alone. You watch the concepts erupting and disappearing. You are apart from concepts, do not identify with them.

Q: I don't have the ability to do that.

M: If you are not, where are the concepts? Where is the question of ignorance or knowledge if you are not there? That primary concept "I Am" hangs on to the body as its identity, hence all the trouble. Will you ever come to the conclusion that you are not the concept?

February 28, 1981

Maharaj: When the body was formed you did not bring any information with you. Later on you collected information externally, and on that basis you are full of pride and conduct your dealings. Did you bring any information with you, right from the beginning?

Questioner: No, I had no information.

M: If you had no information, who is the customer for all this now? You have the primary information that you are which sprouted spontaneously in you — that was your primary capital and all this further mischief is because of that primary information. Is it not so?

Q: That is true, yes.

M: Do you understand what it is, to have your own being, to be?

Q: I do not clearly understand.

M: It is not to be understood through words. Whatever knowledge you derive out of words is ignorance only. To *be* is not to be *understood,* it *is.*

Q: It is just a feeling.

M: Who knows the consciousness?

Q: Consciousness knows itself.

M: Consciousness understanding consciousness — by this method you will not have emancipation. You have to ask yourself, "Who knows this beingness?" If I know that I am, at a particular point, then it means that prior to that point I did not know that I am. That which was not aware of Its existence became aware of Its existence when the consciousness came, and this consciousness is only the nature of the physical body — it is made of material and is therefore temporary.

Q: There is no knowledge in the Absolute?

M: All knowledge is only in the grasp of the five senses and words. Suppose these three, the waking state, deep sleep, and the knowledge "I Am" are not there — what are you?

Q: Just knowingness, consciousness?

M: Is this knowingness, consciousness, in your association continuously, forever?

Q: No.

M: Then give it up. Why do you lean on that which will not be in your association eternally?

All our scriptures say that only the *Parabrahman* is the truth, nothing else is, and you are That eternally.

Q: Why did I separate myself from That?

M: When nothing else but That prevails, how can you be separate from It?

Q: There is a poem written by Jnanaswara to that 1400 year old Sage; one line says, "The vision of knowledge becomes weaker and weaker." What is the meaning of that?

M: The vision of consciousness will also drop off in the ultimate analysis, because knowledge and ignorance are in the realm of consciousness.

Q: *I do not want to let go of a single word of yours.*

M: How long are you going to hang on to words and the meaning of words? How long?

Q: *They are useful so long as the "I Am" is there.*

M: This "I Am" is a concept also, is it not? And you want to hang on to this concept also. This "I Amness" is not going to remain in your association, and when it goes, everything relating to that "I Amness" goes. When this is the state of affairs, what is the use of trying to gain or assimilate knowledge?

Words are not exactly applicable; I have seen exactly how I am not. In the absence of "I Am," what that state is, I have seen, or am seeing, therefore I don't lose anything. In that state there is no question of seeing or experiencing, but for the sake of communication we have to borrow these words.

These are great men, full of wisdom, profound; but how do I look at them? They are just like me. This one is a legal luminary and a Sanskrit scholar; with the combined effect he is trying to capture *Parabrahman* in his words. He is very good at it, but what is the gain?

Q: *To realize that my state is without concepts, that itself is the gain.*

M: You are standing on a concept "I Am," and trying to paint that with another concept.

Q: *This is a different kind of court, the lawyer is hauled into the dock.*

March 1, 1981

Questioner: *Is this "I Amness" which everybody has the same thing as consciousness?*

Maharaj: Other than this consciousness and "I Amness," what is there that can claim "I Am?"

Understand that this "I" is not different at different levels. As the Absolute it is the "I" which in manifesting needs a form. The same Absolute "I" becomes the manifested "I" and in the manifested "I" it is the consciousness which is the source of everything. In the manifested state it is the Absolute with consciousness.

You may think that you consider yourself to be the consciousness, but you generally keep on wanting something as an entity, even if it is spiritual knowledge. The body is only an instrument by which consciousness manifests itself; it has no separate, autonomous identity.

This body, which you love so much, is time-bound and this consciousness, which depends on the material body, is also time-bound.

The vital breath is the active element which keeps the body in action. Consciousness is the passive element. The vital breath will leave the body after a certain span of time and leave dead material; the consciousness will also leave the body and merge with the universal consciousness. This is the normal process — within this what is it you consider yourself to be? This is merely a functioning, there is no separate entity. Actually our true identity is known to everyone, there is no doubt about it. But because of identification with the body as an entity what is definitely known to us is being forgotten.

Listening to what I say may give you a temporary sense of peace and pleasure, but so long as you consider yourself a separate entity wanting spiritual salvation, all this is useless.

There is no entity that can benefit from the listening that takes place. What is birth after all? Birth is only the waking state, deep sleep and sex; suppose the sex is removed, then there will be no interest. The sex cannot fill your stomach, cannot provide you with food, but that is necessary. It is easier to understand that the entire manifestation is of the nature of a dream, or a mirage, but you interpret the rest of the manifestation as being a mirage and won't let go of the seer of the phenomenon. The seer is also part of the mirage.

March 6, 1981

Maharaj: If you have any questions I will try to answer them. This moment now, of this particular situation, is a very peculiar one. You need not talk if you don't want to, you may merely sit. Merely sitting here, at this particular time, will be of great benefit. The moment . . . the auspicious symptom, and it will give the most amazing results . . . incredible . . . this moment itself, this touch of "I Amness" is just a pinprick, just a touch.

If you apperceive what I have said, there is no reason to visit me again. What I have told you is not something to be wondered over or pondered over for a period of time — it is a matter to be apperceived immediately.

Have you had this way of expounding knowledge anywhere else, in quietude?

Questioner: At Ramanasram. Everybody was silent there too.

M: How long were you with Ramana?

Q: Only a short while. How is it that I have been so fortunate as to find Maharaj now?

M: Something good you have done in your past life. If you had not done your homework you would not have visited this place. The rare, lucky ones will visit this place and listen to the talks.

Q: I am having different experiences of warmth, seeing light, and I am afraid.

M: Don't worry about any experiences, try to abide in the experiencer. The experiences are good indications of your development, but don't stagnate at the level of experience.

Q: I usually feel that I am this or that, but I am losing this. I am feeling more detached, not interested in the world. During the experience of the shedding away of these concepts I feel a sense of death and fear.

M: Yes, it will go on like that. So long as you are, such things are bound to happen. You have to transcend the "I Am." If you are alert, focusing your attention on the moment, the "I Am" is a continuous moment, you transcend the "I Am."

March 8, 1981

Questioner: Can we understand our real nature through consciousness? Can we grasp it?

Maharaj: Is there any other instrument through which you can understand your true nature? Whatever is can be perceived by all, *is* perceived by all. Who wants to grasp it? You, as a separate entity, want to know That which is, as the Absolute. It can't be done, because you are the Absolute.

Where does the one who has attained *samadhi* go? The seeker himself has disappeared.

Q: If the seeker is a concept, then the Guru is also a concept.

M: Yes, but that Guru is the support for all seeking. So long as there is word there is seeker; when the word vanishes, there is nothing.

I have experienced all four kinds of speech and transcended them. Rarely will anybody follow this hierarchy to stabilize in the consciousness and transcend consciousness. Starting from *vaikhara* (word), normally we listen to words; from *vaikhari* we go to *madhyama* (mind-thought); in watching the mind we are in *pashayanti* where the concept formation takes place and from there to *Para* (I Am — without words), and finally from *Para* to prior to consciousness. This is the line to follow, but only a rare one follows it — receding, reversing.

Q: Is deep sleep and the state prior to the "I Am" one and the same?

M: As a concept it is the same thing; until you become That, then there will be no one to know. Not only that, but whatever actions are done — whether through you or me — are originally done within that state of deep sleep. In sleep you dream; this being-awake state is the primary dream; the dream in the sleeping state is the secondary dream — it is the transformation of the primary dream. In this state of consciousness, in the primary dream, the entire universe is created and when it is realized that it is a dream — then you are awake. Both dreams are consciousness.

Q: Then the actor cannot know that he is dreaming?

M: That is exactly the beauty of *maya,* the whole heart of it. Understand that the basis of whatever dream it is, is consciousness.

March 9, 1981

Maharaj: This sense of entity that one has, which has been created by the mind, when the consciousness itself disappears, what happens to that sense of entity? Is there anyone who knows that he is dead? It is only the others who say that he is dead.

If the consciousness and the mind were the ultimate truth, then all those millions of forms which have been created and destroyed would have the knowledge of their existence.

In this country, in this life, you acquire something, but the rule of the land is that whatever has been acquired cannot be taken out of the country. Whatever you acquire is because of consciousness, but the law of the land of this life is that nothing can be taken away, once consciousness disappears, everything is gone.

How does man behave in the world? He forgets what it is that is really functioning. He forgets that the forms are only instruments for the functioning of consciousness. He considers himself an entity and spends his whole life working hard, trying to achieve something. The motivation for all this is the sense of me and mine. All kinds of forms are being created and destroyed continuously — that is part of the functioning.

Questioner: *If there is nothing to be achieved by an entity, then what is the purpose of this spiritual seeking?*

M: What is to be understood is — all that is functioning is the consciousness — no entity is involved.

Q: Then what is the use of understanding?

M: There is no benefit for any supposed entity. There should be no sense of even a benefit out of this understanding. You are the understanding. Who is to get the benefit? That which apprehends this has no shape or form.

The forms are created from the five elements — at the end of their span of time they are destroyed. If you live for hundreds of years, nothing will be of any benefit to you.

I have obviously understood all of this and yet I have made sufficient provision for my new flat to be constructed. Understand what might appear as contradiction, but there is no contradiction so long as one sees all this as part of total functioning. Will this appear to any normal person as something reasonable?

Q: Can Maharaj tell us how the different traps can be separated and avoided.

M: You had better get some hefty people to cut up the five elements into little bits — then you will have this separation. It is just one. Consciousness itself is the trap.

Forget all your other questions, merely concentrate on the source of this consciousness because of which everything else is. How did this body arrive, and within it this consciousness which is latent? Find out the source of this.

Q: Maharaj has brought us back to the root.

M: I threw you at the root and buried you, and in that state in which I have buried you, there is nothing to be known, because in that state, consciousness is not. Once this is clearly apperceived, so long as the body is there life must go on, but life appears merely as a series of entertainments.

You should understand from what standpoint I am talking; if you understand you take it, otherwise you leave it. Nobody in the world will tell you so bluntly. When you really, intuitively, understand what I mean, then you will come to the end of spirituality.

March 10, 1981

Questioner: Why does the identification seem to change constantly?

Maharaj: In consciousness the identification with an individual will keep on changing, but once the identity is lost it is possible to remain in total manifestation.

Q: Can I reach the Absolute state while consciousness is there?

M: In that state there is no one to be conscious so there is no question of reaching that state as long as consciousness is present.

Q: But I thought Maharaj said . . .

M: That state is where knowledge is absorbed in knowledge, and knowledge is not aware of itself. The instrument has to be there and consciousness is the instrument. In consciousness, consciousness is conscious of itself, but in the state prior to the arising of consciousness, who is there and with what instrument can one be conscious?

In that state which is not tainted by anything there is no conditioning. Take the example of space. In space there is darkness and light, the space is there whether darkness or light is there; in the same way the state prior to consciousness is always there. Right now it is there. It is the substratum of everything. A *jnani* is one who abides in that state of space in spite of body and mind.

Q: What is the practice, is it meditation only?

M: You must possess that confirmation that you are formless, designless; not only rely on meditation. Always insist that you are formless, free, and are not conditioned. You must hammer on this constantly, that is the practice.

Q: I have longer times when I am disassociated from the body-mind. I don't understand what is happening to me when I see the body act and feel outside of it.

M: What is wrong with that? You must have a strong conviction; that conviction means practicing. That conviction means not only "I Am," but it means I am free from "I Am" also.

You know you are, without words. Just be that. You are not to think or imagine anything. Before it occurs to you that something is, you must *be*. You must be there in order to meditate. When you wake up the first thing in the morning, at that moment you know only you *are*, emerging from deep sleep to a waking state. Later on you think I am so and so, etc.

Q: In meditation I hear sounds and see visions.

M: To hear something you must be there. That state is a most Godly state but it is more important to be your Self.

Q: There is always fear.

M: The fear is because of ignorance. It is not external sound, it is the manifestation of your consciousness. The Godly illumination is there provided the Self-effulgence is there. To see the God, you must be there. To get to know the knower is difficult; it is something like knowing a township; it is not individualistic, it is manifestation.

When you are that manifest consciousness state, it is something like . . . a deep dark blue state; you are in that homogenous, deep dark blue state. That is the first step of beingness. From that deep dark blue Self-effulgent homogenous state into no-knowingness state — that is your true identity. It is a no-knowingness state, a total, complete, perfect state. In that knowingness state everything is imperfect, is is never complete — that is why you want more and more. In spite of plenteousness, the knowingness state is incomplete.

Q: What is the effect at death?

M: The effect is upon those who know that the person is dead and gone. There is no effect on the one who is dead and gone — he doesn't know he is dead and gone. The body is made of food, the true you is not in this body.

A lot can be said, but you will not be able to receive what I say. Suppose I say that if you are not, the Brahman is not — will you understand? You are so much obsessed by death because of your identification with the body. Because you are thinking of death, death is sure for you, but if you are the Self there is no question of death for you.

March 11, 1981

Questioner: By reading the book of Maharaj's talks, I feel great freedom and joy, I think I am experiencing the living word.

Maharaj: What is it which was experiencing this? It was the sense of presence.

Q: I have read so many books, but this was a new revelation, a new experience. Why don't I get the same experience from other books?

M: I am not going to accept any of your compliments. Your questions are from the body-mind level and you will accept the answers on the same level. You are riding the horse of body-identification.

Q: I wanted to know why I got such experiences from reading your book and not from others.

M: I am not interested in your experiences; I am interested only in you. The talker and the listener are one. Most of the others who come here may be said to be in a state similar to that of having had a really good dinner; they have had their fill, and now they are chewing the cud, like a cow — they are not interested in further food. That is why there are no questions. If someone like you doesn't arrive and ask questions, there will be no questions. You have come to seek knowledge and you are knowledge.

Q: Dakshinamurti taught his disciples in silence.

M: Hang Dakshinamurti! That is hearsay, something you have read or heard. What is your experience? I am here and you are here: ask questions.

Q: Why is it that some die young and others live a long life?

M: Will there be birth or death without the consciousness or self? When you say they die young or live long, those that are born, actually what logic does the Self know? Does the sun know when it sets or rises? First understand what it is that is born and then this mystery will be solved.

Q: The body is born, the Self is not born.

M: If the Self is not there, can the body be born? What do you understand by the word birth? Are you born?

Q: As long as we identify with the body we are born.

M: I talk only to the consciousness about the consciousness, the common man will not understand.

Q: What is the way to understand? What is there to do? The quickest way?

M: Understanding and being in that true nature is the task. There is no other God than this sense of presence and I am this sense of presence. Understanding this with conviction is the quickest way. Understand that original state when there was none other. That is true knowledge, my true nature. Plenty of *avatars* have come and gone, but that space is there all the time.

Q: How does one overcome basic ignorance?

M: What is it that understands there is something like ignorance?

Q: Knowledge understands.

M: Understand that you are that knowledge and forget about ignorance. Any beautiful music, when it is heard, any dancing girl, when she dances — if by all this nobody is moved, he is either a *jnani* or a donkey. Here is a roomful of such people who will not be moved by the beauty of anything. I am in that state where there is total absence of any concept of presence or absence. You are also in that state, but you don't know it. My consciousness is not very effective; there is no recognition now of anybody as an individual, a person. If you feel like sitting you are welcome; whenever you feel like going you can go.

March 14, 1981

Questioner: By the grace of Maharaj I find that now my eyes are able to see and my ears are able to hear.

Maharaj: What the eyes see and the ears hear is only the false. Both will disappear. You are That which witnesses.

What is understood and practiced by the common Hindu man as spirituality is that water from the river is carried in a vessel and poured over an image of God. Some of these images have been placed so that one has to climb 500 steps to reach them. This is considered to bring great merit. They collect water in brass vessels in Benares from the Ganges. They carry that water, walking all the way, to South India, to Rameshwara, and pour it over the idol, and they will take the sea water from Rameshwara back to Benares and pour it over the head of the idol there. This is their concept of liberation — water is taken from one place and carried to another — what a strenuous concept!

Q: What we hear at the feet of Maharaj is something that is ever new.

M: What I am telling you about can never be new or old — it is unchanging, everlasting.

This consciousness in which concepts arise is itself a concept, and so long as consciousness remains all other concepts will continue to arise.

The Absolute unmanifest is what Is. Whatever we think about that Absolute state can only be a concept, until the consciousness ends and we are in that Absolute state.

One achieves something and one guards it, but how long can you guard it? Only until you are in deep sleep. You have a fond concept and you hang on to it all day; in deep sleep where is that concept?

Q: How does Maharaj talk to us if he does not accept individuality?

M: The sun does not shine for individuals. The words come out of the consciousness, spontaneously, as part of the total functioning. There are any number of experiences, some of them you like and you keep them in your memory and pamper them — that itself is suffering. All your experiences should be just part of the total functioning, happening spontaneously.

March 15, 1981

Maharaj: I am not inclined to collect more people and expound knowledge because I am not able to deliver myself as something tangible to you. Krishnamurti is talking, I am also talking — there is no substance in that. You are recording the talks and writing it down — in the final analysis, there is no substance in that.

Once it is realized that it is only a total functioning of the manifest consciousness and there is no individual entity, there will be no question of liberation, of birth or death, or of a doer doing anything.

Normally, in the name of spirituality, knowledge is expounded. Knowledge is in the realm of the five elements and it is talked about as real or unreal as long as the knowledge "I Am" is there; it is a product of the knowledge "I Am."

A *jnani* is that state from which witnessing of the knowledge "I Am" takes place. In that *jnani* state there is no touch of "I Amness" (it is a quality-less state) and it is not knowledge — knowledge means "I Amness." Suppose there are no thoughts, time has stopped, but space will be there. A thought-free state is something like space, space-like. I am the witness that the thought-free state is there, that is the Self, "I Am," the being. Because the being is there, having removed all the pollution, including thought, time is also gone and space and beingness is there. When that state ends, it is the Absolute state, a something sweet-like state. You are just playing with words and the meaning of words — you don't go to the root from where the words emanate. Nobody goes to the root; they are fascinated by the display. When the support of the body-mind is not available, what are you then like?

I am in the state beyond suffering and enjoyment. It is said that when knowledge is realized, the devotion persists still but actually there is no personality left. There is no question of devotion; devotion to whom? However, they say that devotion is there — it might be for the guidance of other seekers.

March 16, 1981

Maharaj: Even in the highest Saints there is always some doubt about the clarity of "I Am," and this enquiry of what I am must be gone into at any and all levels. The importance and significance of the enquiry is that no one can give you an answer to this enquiry except yourself. Each one, as "I," has to find out what this "I" is. The merest description that can be given to this consciousness is that it is as fine, as subtle, as space. In maturity your consciousness is God.

That original state, prior to the arising of consciousness, cannot be described, one can only *be* That.

I keep on repeating that whatever one listens to ultimately means nothing — because whatever I am, that is exactly what you are.

Any action that one takes depends on a certain image that one has about oneself, and that image remains only so long as consciousness is there. Is this clearly understood?

People come here with a certain set of concepts; I hold the mirror before them of what they are as phenomena and ultimately they realize that as phenomena they are nothing and when consciousness departs they will reach their original state — which was there before the body-cum-consciousness arose. In that original state there was no experience, even now any experience that one thinks one has is only a concept.

In that state, before consciousness arose, there was no query of "Who am I?" because there was no one who wanted to know that answer. This question arises only in consciousness; anything in consciousness is only a concept and therefore it has to be wrong.

Out of millions of people, why do only some come here? Obviously it is when consciousness has this enquiry in consciousness that it brings people here.

Questioner: Is the "I Am" a concept or the only reality?

M: "I Am" is only a few letters. Has anyone been able to keep this "I Am" in his pocket for all time?

Q: I am — but without words?

M: Yes. If whoever feels this "I Am" had knowledge, would he have cared to become this "I Am"? No, he would have said, "I don't want this consciousness."

Q: I understand.

M: You are unreal — you know that you are — that is also unreal. This sense of presence is an untruth; it is like a dream.

Q: How can this "I Amness" be the source of misery?

M: Try to find out when this concept of happiness and unhappiness arose. It was not there until I had this consciousness.

Everybody loves this sense of presence and wants it to continue for all time but they don't go further into the past and find out whose ecstasy created this sense of presence. Because of some physical ecstasy, lasting only for an instant, this speck of consciousness in which the entire universe is contained has come into existence.

Q: I don't feel the misery of "I Amness"; I feel that everything is right. Does it mean that I don't want to look at the misery?

M: You cannot do anything — you have to enjoy what is — is it not so? To suffer or to enjoy, you have no choice.

Nevertheless, experiences will be there. You may not be involved in the experiences, but so long as the "I Am" is there, experiences will be there. The magic, the art, of this consciousness is that it has not only hidden the fact that it is the source of all misery, but has made itself the source of all apparent happiness.

March 17, 1981

Questioner: What does Maharaj mean by Linga-deha?

Maharaj: It is the seed, the chemical, the product of the five elemental essences which give rise to and sustain the consciousness "I Am." Just like the seed of a tree, that seed latently contains all future manifestations and expressions of the tree that will sprout out of that seed. You take a fountain pen and on the paper you put a drop of ink, so that drop is the *Linga-deha*. That drop is the moment of conception; its expression is the thought-free state, like space, in the knowingness state. That is the quality of knowingness, space-like; there is no concept, but its expression is the physical, tangible. Just imagine it is infinitesimal, but its expression is manifest infinity.

Foreigners understand, but when the Indians come, they listen to the talks, but they are still attached to all their bodily relatives.

At *Linga-deha* level, when you worship your Guru, you are the expression of Guru, in so many ways. You will be experiencing so many things at such a level, but all that has emanated out of you only, out of your love and devotion for Guru, and finally, as you evolve, all those expressions merge into you. This is very important, this is the consummation of devotion or *Saguna Bhakti*.

That *Linga-deha,* that little drop, and the knowledge "I Am" is the same. What we see is the manifest world which appears in that speck of consciousness. As sweetness is the nature of sugar, so this speck of consciousness is the nature of that drop of *Linga-deha.* The parents, the source of the *Linga-deha,* are merely an excuse for preparing that which was conceived. Your true state was there before the body and consciousness arose, is there now and will be there after the body and consciousness go. Somebody may challenge what I am saying.

I have never had any doubt about what you are or who you are, because I have understood my true state — what I am, I know you are.

Some people will spread this illumination, but it will be the foreigners, not the Indians. At a later date people will question, "Was there really such a person who expounded knowledge in this way?"

March 18, 1981

Maharaj: There is no duality between the Guru and the *Bhakta.* In That which Is there is no duality, has never been any duality. The word *Bhakta* means devotion, but in actuality it indicates togetherness, one only, unity.

Questioner: The flame of devotion lights my way.

M: Who speaks about that flame? When we talk we don't talk about a person, but about that dynamic, manifest flame "I Am."

Q: That is not extinguishable.

M: Who says that?

Q: *I believe that.*

M: Because it is your belief, is it right?

Q: *I have no proof.*

M: You are running. Who talks about the proof? With your faith, whatever you are worshipping and devoted to, that you will get.

The trouble about your spirituality is that you are listening only to that knowledge about Iswara which is useful to an entity, you are collecting only that knowledge. As a man, an entity, this is a temporary phase of your emotions, or sentiments. No person will be able to conserve his personality or his identity forever. That guiding principle is not a person. Nowadays I don't expound any theme of spirituality. I don't even talk, but still, why the attraction which brings you here? With this I develop my encumbrances. I have nothing to gain in this bargain except these encumbrances.

Do you know the ingredients of that personality? Unless you get to know that fully, you will not go beyond.

Q: *What about my desires, my needs?*

M: You are in need of your Self.

Q: *Is there any involvement between my desires and the raw material?*

M: Plenty of involvement. Out of the interaction and play of the five elements this food body is available, in that the fragrance and taste is the knowledge "I Am." Now you find out what is the indication that you are in this food body.

Q: *Would fasting help me to find my Self?*

M: Not at all. That "I Amness" is the very expression of the food. Suppose you want to find sweetness, sweetness is the quality of sugar, if you reject sugar where is the sweetness?

Q: *Then I always have to go outside myself to food, to get this taste?*

M: Can you get the food from inside? The supply comes from outside.

Q: *I have always been led to believe that this sense of presence did not depend on body, that is the essence of spirituality, and now you tell me the opposite!*

M: Therefore understand this mystery itself. Where does the world exist? It exists in this speck of consciousness, and this consciousness can exist only if there is food.

Whatever life you are living, you are only entertaining a concept. Find out is there such a thing as an individual. Think over it.

If the entertainment of the experience is easy, if it pleases you, you call it happiness, if not you call it unhappiness.

The feeling that you are — the sense of presence — what has caused it to come about? Think on it.

Q: Everything is happening because I am.

M: Will you be able to retain this understanding always?

Q: Just for a moment and then the identification comes back.

M: It's a long way to get the understanding stabilized that everything is happening because I Am. Now, for how many days will you be in India?

Q: I have only a few more days here.

M: It is not important where you are, once you are established in the "I Am." It is like space — it neither comes nor goes; just as when you demolish the walls of a building only space remains.

March 20, 1981

Maharaj: My personality, or individuality, is thrown to the winds, it is no more there. What you are visiting is only that Duhkha Bhagavan, the God of Sorrow. Bhagavan is this manifestation, but sorrow only. It is not involved in thought or activities — it is just the manifestation. I am the total functioning and whatever in the functioning, at the moment, has certain significance, that I am.

It is only by taking the aid of this consciousness, which is suffering, that I am talking. This kind of experience happens only to a very rare one. Don't ask anything, just listen.

This consciousness, this manifestation, this functioning, has no shape, form or color.

Questioner: Would Maharaj explain more about Duhkha Bhagavan?

M: Duhka means pain, suffering, agony. *Bhagavan* means not only God, it is indicative of explosiveness, a flash . . . an explosive flash . . . world perception — with the appearance of "I Amness."

When there is an explosion of fireworks there is a crashing sound, a flash of light, and lighting up of the surrounding area. Similarly the "I Am" explodes into being and the whole perceptible universe is conjured up, but consciousness, the "I Amness," gives rise to inadequacy, imperfection, and therefore the beginning of sorrow, misery, etc., and the settling into body-mind sense. From perfect to imperfect — from no-being to being. In the reverse direction — from body-mind to beingness to Absolute — then the consciousness state is a Godly state.

Q: Why is there so much pain and unhappiness in this world?

M: Because you are always in search of happiness. Happiness and unhappiness are interrelated. If you did not have unhappiness, how would you recognize happiness?

March 23, 1981

Maharaj: I am That which represents the absence of what is seen. If you try to accommodate what I say within this concept that you are a human being, it cannot be done. In spite of listening to all I have said, most of you will continue to identify yourself as a body, and you will look on me as an individual, but I am not that. My real presence is the absence of the phenomena that you see.

My sleep is not the kind you have, it is pure consciousness. When I sleep there is awareness of total manifestation and also the Unmanifest. There is no distinction between an individual and the total universe.

You think that I am ill but that is because you identify me with the body. I consider this illness as an extraordinary state which comes to the lot of a rare one so long as the individuality exists in the form of a body — but the importance of that is impossible to describe. That state is full of suffering; nevertheless, it is full of significance and it comes to a rare one.

The question of what one is comes only in manifestation, in comparison with other phenomena. In my state there is no phenomenon; my existence is prior to any manifestation. There is no question of who or what I am.

Questioner: Would Maharaj repeat what was said earlier about that state where there is no phenomenon?

M: Once it is said it is gone. The correct way of listening is to concentrate on the words which reveal your own identity, forget all other things. You arrive at your identity as that state which was prior to words. Words cannot satisfy That.

This consciousness, because of which everything else is, is itself merely the light of That which is, a reflection of That which is. The average person who considers himself a seeker worships the various concepts, not his true being.

Q: Would Maharaj talk some more about the state which was prior to consciousness?

M: What is the point? Anything you can think of that state is only a concept and that concept will last only so long as the consciousness is there.

Only the experiencer remains — unsmeared by any experiences — even the experience of remaining.

I am nothing but how dare I talk like this? Because I know none of the experiences have remained with me.

You will not find anyone so blunt as I. Everyone is concerned with these experiences from birth to death but no one gives any thought to that state before experiencing began. One who has a clear understanding of this consciousness cannot attach any importance to any experience.

Q: I want to give up this identity with the body, I want to find out who I am. How do I go about it?

M: If you do not have the knowledge "I Am" who is going to seek? You must be, only then can the search begin. Remember the knowledge "I Am" — that alone pervades everything — be only that, give up the rest.

Q: When I think "I Am," then immediately come thoughts of the things that I am. I know that comes from the mind.

M: Before you think — you are. In the space all movement happens, for any appearance or any movement, the space must be there.

For the question "Who am I" there is no reply, but you may reply any way you like, you can give it any name or title you like.

People do not go to the root-meaning of whatever is heard or read, they just repeat, parrot-like. I take a serious objection to people just reciting the *bhajans,* parrot-like.

How many people have understood the meaning of certain couplets sung at *bhajans?* The sun and the moon are the reflections of that very principle "I Am."

Spirituality is open and at the same time it is a mystery. Because you are, all the worlds, the universe is; this is your reflection.

If you want to know what you are, that is all given in the *bhajans.* If you close your eyes and almost forget yourself, half-sleep, that is exactly what you are. But if you want to get a glimpse, the first vision that you get is that deep blue space, that is the very idol of beauty, the image of beauty. Very often I have elucidated this point but rarely has anybody been able to catch what I am driving at.

At *bhajans* I used to stress certain couplets by shouting loudly but nobody understood what I was doing. I was stressing certain couplets so that people would go deeper into the meaning of it, but they were only shouting louder! Not only was I loudly stressing that particular line but I used to repeat it. I was inspired to shout those lines at the top of my voice, "You are that speck of consciousness and out of that the entire cosmos is created." I was deeply devoted to the singing of *bhajans* because it was providing all the spiritual nourishment. Whenever I used to strike the profound meaning of a particular *bhajan* I used to dance in the room. I have all the exuberance to dance and sing now, but there is no energy.

After that I never went to any Sage or Saint. However, many Sages and Saints visited me, but unfortunately I did not meet anybody who considered the sun and the moon and the universe as their expression — such a Sage I did not come across.

Q: Although I do not know Marati, I have felt the deeper meaning of the bhajans *intuitively.*

M: Many people do *bhajans* here, but they are not able to grasp the deeper meaning. Many of the foreigners are able to catch the deeper meaning. You (the foreigners) have that advantage because all of you who are interested in this were in your previous incarnation the army of that great incarnation Rama, followers of Rama, so you were already blessed at that time. In further incarnations you migrated to the East; you are more at home in this place than the Indians are.

Foreigners recognize me, but people in the street don't know me, because that great Rama blessed all his army, all his followers, at that time.

I admire the foreigners — not only do they come thousands of miles to be here but they spend so much money to stay in Bombay.

Q: Unless there were that deep urge, we would not come.

M: That is your very destiny. In that chemical which you are, that urge is already planted therein.

You people come here and sit, with determination to get what you want. Therefore I have great respect and great regard for you.

March 25, 1981

Maharaj: Treat the body like a visitor, or guest, which has come and will go. You must know your position as a host very clearly while the guest is still there. What is the exact nature of the host after the guest leaves must be realized while the guest is present. Have you understood? Give me some idea of that position in which you will find yourself when this body guest leaves.

Questioner: *There is no identity.*

M: Good. Is this a firm conviction?

Q: *Yes, in the meditation.*

M: What is the significance of the guest, the sign?

Q: *As soon as the guest comes there is the sense of identity as a host.*

M: The sense of presence, "I Amness," is the sign of the guest. Are your answers out of deep conviction?

Q: *Yes.*

M: Then there is no need to come tomorrow.

Q: *It is only in deep meditation that I know it.*

M: Do you accept completely the knowledge that you do not exist?

Q: *There are moments in meditation when I really feel the conviction.*

M: It is not a firm conviction if it is not there all the time. When one is very sleepy — just at the point of going into deep sleep — at that point he wants nothing else except to go to sleep. Similarly, at the last moment, when the breath is leaving, there is also a moment of ecstasy. At that point, when the life force and consciousness leave, there is that moment of ecstasy, that last moment of knowing. One who has thoroughly apprehended this is a *jnani* to whom there is no question of birth or death.

Even if you hear this and think it is true, the conceptualizing will not stop. Already some concept has begun in you. Whatever I have told you now is only about that speck of "I Amness."

Q: *Would Maharaj tell us more about that moment of death?*

M: Nothing more can be said about it. It is the culmination or termination of the Self experience, "I Am." After the termination of "I Amness" there is no experience of knowingness or not knowingness; the knowingness is the quality of the material stuff. What did you know prior to your birth? Similarly, after death this instrument is missing; without the body there is no experience. Eternity has no birth and no death, but a temporary state has a beginning and an end.

Even when the consciousness goes, you prevail — you always are — as the Absolute. As the consciousness you are everything; whatever is, is you. All this knowledge has dawned on me, I am not that knowledge. The knowledge "I Am," and all its manifestations, are understood. In understanding, I am not That.

March 26, 1981

Maharaj: The only knowledge you will get here is knowledge of the Self; it will not help you to make a living in the world. Do you have any idea of what your true nature is? Since you have understood what you are not, you should no longer be concerned with what you are not. Is that clear?

Questioner: Yes.

M: You still have an idea of what you are but even that image must be totally erased, so that there is no idea of any entity, any identification. Now that you think you have understood what you are, what use will you make of the consciousness? Any use of the consciousness will be for others.

Q: The grace of the Guru is necessary in order to understand.

M: The grace is always there but the receptivity must be there to accept that grace. One must have the firm conviction that what is heard here is the absolute truth.

Instead of becoming impregnated with what I give you, to the extent that you are one with it, you merely accept it, put it in your pocket and keep on using concepts which you have accumulated already. None of you will really understand what I am, you have your own concepts of me.

Q: I have understood with the intellect. What can I do to realize it?

M: There is nothing you, as an entity, can do. That which has taken root will by itself flower into intuitive understanding.

Q: This understanding will take some time.

M: Is this not a concept? The very concept is a hazard. When my Guru told me what the position is, I listened and said, "Oh, this is how it is." And that was that — the end of it.

If there are no more questions I will close the session. I am not here to keep a watch over you. If you really understand what has been said there is no reason to come again, and if you can't understand, then what is the use of continuing?

Q: On occasion there is a spontaneous feeling of universal love; is this based on body-mind, or is it something else?

M: Total love is the very nature of consciousness. When this feeling arises there is nothing you can do — how can one embrace the entire ocean?

March 28, 1981

Questioner: What is the relation between consciousness and the intellect?

Maharaj: Intellect is the expression of consciousness.

Q: We understand and apperceive everything through the intellect only.

M: Things to be done must be done, things to be understood must be understood. Things to be done are normally your present worldly life and these you must carry out. In spirituality you have to *understand,* there is no question of *doing.* In spirituality there is no name and form. Name and form are necessary for your practical worldly life. The one who understands that name and form are not his identity is in spirituality. Presently you are still drawn towards name and form. Your identity in the phenomenal world as name and form is temporary, a passing show, and anything relating to name and form is not going to remain.

One who understands spirituality through various concepts will be caught up in a vicious circle.

If you are caught up in concepts, you will be caught up in the circle of concepts . . . rebirth, reincarnation, these are all concepts. If you are caught up in these concepts you are bound to have them. Out of concepts the forms are created, such as buildings, etc. Originally you make a plan, you have a concept, the concept is born out of you, and you give it a concrete shape, but it remains a concept.

With the experience of so-called birth you are caught up in the cycle like the picture on the TV screen. All this life-happening is something like a cinema.

You must have observed daily that situations are constantly changing — that is the quality or expression of your identity with the body-mind.

It is the consciousness that is playing about, and in that manifest consciousness all these various faces and bodies are playing about. You are not these faces and bodies, you are the consciousness out of which the words are now flowing.

Just as the play you see on the TV or cinema screen is not real, similarly this play is also not real. For a *jnani* all the play is unreal.

I am not going to give you solutions to your family problems, I am telling you how this worldly life is not. After listening to these talks you still want to gain some profit for yourself; that is a pity. How astonishing it is . . . in spite of my discouraging you from coming here, still you come here, how does it happen?

Without making demands we see the dream. Why do we see the dream? Because in deep sleep the consciousness wakes up, spontaneously, and because it woke up, it manifests itself in certain visions.

Just like that, this also, your visiting this place.

I am not talking to you for my advantage, nor are you listening for your advantage — all this language is sprouting spontaneously in a dreamlike state.

I always try to direct you towards the truth but you come here with a bundle of conceptual sticks and stones, and instead of listening to what I say, you play with the sticks and stones — on me.

Right now, think of that last moment when the body will go — at that time with what identity are you going to quit?

This is a fraud, everything is fraudulent, just like a dream world.

Q: What is the primary cause? What was the crime?

M: The crime was that this consciousness started feeling conscious, the mischief started.

Whether you like it or don't like it, I am going to place before you the factual state of affairs. You know you are — but it is all imaginary. You think you are — but it is a fraud. Whatever the nature of the beingness and its behavior, it is not your behavior.

When you abide in your true identity you are out of this michievous dream world. I have placed before you what you are.

All of you have the fear that you are going to die, that this consciousness is going to depart — all the expressions are the expressions of the food essence body, not you. Sweetness or pungency are the expressions of the food, you cannot conserve or preserve them. In the same way this "I Amness" is a quality or expression of the food essence body, and you cannot retain it forever.

March 30, 1981

Maharaj: I am amazed and astonished that you are sitting here. The talk is emanating from a state where there are no words. What identity do you think you have?

Questioner: How to establish oneself firmly in the awareness of "I Am"? Does one think "I Am," "I Am"?

M: Is it necessary to think that you are sitting here? You know that you are sitting here. However loudly and often I urge you not to think and act in terms of an entity, identified with a body, you keep on doing so. Whatever name and form there is belongs to that material, and that material is not you. Do you analyze the problem and with a firm conviction decide that you are not the material? When the material disintegrates, what does the name refer to? Does is have any significance?

Only one in ten million goes to the crux of the matter, analyzes what it is, comes to a conclusion, and gets liberated, all by himself. The one who gets liberated is the consciousness, there is no entity.

The ultimate understanding is that which enables the understanding to take place and itself becomes so subtle, so fine, that it disappears. And when this consciousness arises again, then the *Samadhi* is broken and this "I Amness" starts again.

The words come from the consciousness, and the consciousness needs the strength of the body. The strength of the body is gradually weakening, and therefore the words do not come out as freely as I would like. Spending great energy, I repeat and repeat — but how many have understood? Basically the thing is so simple that I get frustrated when you keep on coming here, listen to what I say, and show no indication that the words have reached home.

What is the birth principle? You have understood or you have not understood. If you have understood, why do you keep on coming? If you have not understood, why do you keep coming?

Q: Maharaj, I just like being here with you.

M: That is a different thing — but have you really imbibed what I want you to understand?

Q: We come here with so many concepts and what you are teaching is so astounding that it is like a shock treatment. So how do you expect us to ask questions? Let us absorb the shock for some time, then the questions will come. We are stunned into silence.

M: Those who come here and listen to my talks and understand will become the Gurus when they return to their own countries.

It is so easy to understand, why don't you understand? At the present time, in manifestation, what you are is the consciousness, and the consciousness cannot remain unless the food body is there; therefore consciousness depends on the food body — which is essentially of an ephemeral nature — and I cannot be that. It's as simple as that; why don't you understand?

It must happen that the consciousness is no longer conscious of itself. The sweetness is in the sugar and I am the one who understands and tastes the sweetness. All these spiritual concepts have come in conventionally. The last step is — knowingness in its ultimate state is no-knowingness. Transcending consciousness is when the consciousness knows and understands the consciousness.

Q: This morning, between deep sleep and awakening, there was this quiet, for the fraction of a moment, when there was a complete knowing, a stillness, just being-ness.

M: It is quite an elevated state, but don't get caught up only in that. Deep sleep is something like a block of ice; nothing is there, now it is again reshaping, the warmth is taking place, and with that warmth you feel that you are.

In the playing of the flute, the whole world is fascinated. The consciousness has kept you entranced in the play of the world. Enquire about that flute and who is playing it. Go to the source.

Q: When you are living this life a number of questions arise and we have to be constantly aware of the consciousness, but the mind won't let us.

M: The mind is an instrument for communication, for practical purposes. The mind cannot grasp the truth. The Self witnesses the mind, but the mind cannot catch hold of the Self.

March 31, 1981

Maharaj: When a clear understanding takes place of the nature and function of consciousness, that understanding no longer needs consciousness, because that understanding becomes the knower of consciousness.

Questioner: Is it possible to function as the total manifestation, not as an individual?

M: What do you understand to be the total manifestation and individual?

Q: What is manifestation?

M: I am the manifestation. I, the Absolute unmanifested, am the same "I" manifested. Consciousness is the expression of the Absolute, there are not two.

Q: If my life gives me great satisfaction and happiness, why should I bother about what or who I am?

M: This consciousness will not rest until it gets the answer. This consciousness cannot bear its own existence, cannot bear its own consciousness.

Q: It wants to go back to its own place of rest.

M: I am not inclined to discuss with words.

You people come here with steadfastness, diligently you come here and sit. If you have such a liking, you are welcome.

My teaching is very simple; the experiencer and the experiences are all fancies.

When you are a young person you like all the activities of a young person very much, you get very involved in them; once youth goes you are disinterested in the activities of a young person. Similarly, as long as you are wearing this concept "I Am" you will be involved with all the concepts. When this concept "I Am" departs there will be no memory left that *I was* and *I had* those experiences: the very memory will be erased. Before you are completely liquidated, while there are some traces left of you, it would be better to quit this place.

You may not come across these teachings in such great detail, and at this level.

This lady has piled up a lot of knowledge, she possesses stacks of it, but in due course she will not only forget whatever she has piled up, but she will forget herself, that she was.

April 4, 1981

Questioner: Is a Self-realized person always in a state of bliss?

Maharaj: One who has transcended the body idea does not need the *ananda* (bliss). When you didn't have experience of the body, you were in that blissful state. That state which is prior to your birth cannot be described as deep sleep, it is beyond that. The experience of the *jnani* is the same as your state prior to birth, it is a complete state.

Q: How can I be That?

M: You are in that state all the time, prior to having the body, but you are confused because of the body consciousness.

Q: The body is there.

M: Don't ask questions, just listen. You need the company of the Sages to understand what I am saying. This knowledge cannot be understood by the intellect.

Q: Is there sat-chit-ananda *in the eternal state?*

M: The food essence is *sattwa,* and the quality of that is consciousness, and inside that is the *sat-chit-ananda* (being-consciousness-bliss). The eternal state is prior to that.

Q: I have read in the books that the main reason to be born is your own desire to be born; how can it fit in with the state before birth?

M: Your birth is the result of the desire of your parents.

Q: How can I be released from bondage?

M: There is no bondage at all, bondage is imaginary. If you are oriented towards the consciousness all your questions will be dissolved by your Self.

Q: What is the obstacle to my realizing this?

M: The only bondage is your constant memory that you are the body.

Q: Without understanding fully what Maharaj is, still people come here. Why is that?

M: That is the union of knowledge and that principle which transcends knowledge. There is attraction between these two. That is why people from all over the world come here.

I am intangible, you cannot add to me or take away from me. I am full, complete in all respects. Whatever you do to me, you will have to suffer yourself. If you are angry with me, you have to suffer. If you do anything to me, it will rebound upon you. If you spit at the sky, the spit will fall on you only.

Q: What is the material world created from?

M: Out of the manifest consciousness, the material world is created — the eternal *Parabrahman,* the eternal Brahman, in which this play is always going on. In that play you are the total, no separate identity arises. In the body is the taste of "I Am," — when the body is gone, the taste is gone. When you have some problem you refer to a book. Why don't you investigate yourself — find out what you are.

In this play of the five elements, whatever is seen or experienced is merely enjoyment, and for this enjoyment, or entertainment, mind is very necessary.

Q: What are Brahma, Vishnu, and the other Gods?

M: They are merely appearances in consciousness. Each appearance has its own duration. That duration may be for millions of years, but they are all appearances and have an alloted span of existence.

The knower of the knowledge is not affected in any way by the individual hopes, fears, etc.

April 10, 1981

Maharaj: The Unmanifest ever exists but this manifest knowingness arises and departs. Presently I do not have any individuality — what is available is only the consciousness for the expression of which this material instrument is available. This consciousness is not a very desirable thing, it is an imperfect state.

There is no reason or law of cause and effect for the functioning of this universal consciousness. Why something happens at a particular time cannot be explained in this dualistic state. We can only watch the functioning and cannot ask for any reason for any functioning which takes place. If we had the choice of taking on this body-cum-consciousness, who would be foolish enough to accept it? It is only because there has been no choice, everything has been spontaneous. The suffering also has to be taken on because it is part of the total functioning, and there is no entity who can pick and choose.

There is no individuality left; nevertheless, so long as this body is part of the total functioning, whatever comes in the total functioning has to be suffered. There is any amount of suffering in the total functioning — this body is one of the millions of forms and the share of this body from the total suffering has to be experienced.

Questioner: I am trying to understand this.

M: You are hanging onto an entity that is trying to understand. All of this is simply for the sake of communication. Who is an entity trying to understand what?

You are carrying on a lot of activities because of certain concepts you entertain, to satisfy the concepts that have arisen spontaneously in you. All this process of communication, expounding, etc., will go on so long as this conscious presence is available, and all this merely to satify the concept "I Am," and you, the Absolute, are not the primary concept "I Am."

I am telling you all this and probably you like it, you enjoy it — but it is almost impossible for you to assimilate or perceive what I am saying. I am sure you have not understood exactly what I am saying. These are two great personalities, legal pundits. By coming here and listening to my talks how can they put to use their legal knowledge?

April 13, 1981

Questioner: *The disciple is devoted to the Guru; is this not duality?*

Maharaj: In the world duality always exists. Manifestation can only take place in duality because of the identification with the body-mind. If the Guru and the disciple are not identified with the body, where does the question of duality arise? The pupil and the Guru are only knowledge and there is no form or design to knowledge.

Q: *We have accepted that we are not the body, that we were never born and cannot die, but it seems that something is missing; what is it?*

M: Give me a sample of the one who has heard and accepted. I assume that those who listen to me are knowledge.

An animal exists only to appease the hunger; is that all you are here for? There must be a change in you after listening to me all these days. One has to know that one is not the *form* but the *consciousness* which gives sentience to the form. Has this change really occurred?

Q: *The Guru explains that the attachment to the Guru is also a concept; how to get rid of it? The* sadhaka *wants to pay his respects to the Guru all the time.*

M: This is initial stage talk — duality is there. The *sadhaka* considers Guru as something other than himself, so he wants to pay his respects. The *sadhaka* is also a Guru, a *jnani,* there is no difference.

I am still doing this *puja* for *my* Guru. It has to be maintained for the guidance of others; unless you have respect and love for a Guru the process of your becoming concept-free will not be hastened. If you understand what I say, only then do you come here. If nobody comes, I will not be unhappy; whatever must happen has already happened.

April 15, 1981

Questioner: Would realization be possible by hearing the truth from the Guru or is there any other way?

Maharaj: No, only with the Grace and guidance of the Guru. The Guru is the one who knows totally what is qualitative Brahman and non-qualitative, what is mundane matter and what is spiritual matter. You are holding on to all these things you have heard here as concepts. You don't try to be that. You like knowledge as a concept.

Q: Maharaj has said that the inner Guru is more important than the outer Guru.

M: In the initial stages you must have an external Guru. That Guru initiates you with the inner Guru.

Q: What are mantras *for?*

M: A *mantra* is indicative of the aim or object in you.

Q: I am a physician and I sometimes get attached to my patients and involved in their problems. Sometimes I can be detached and not feel involved, but my patients are like warriors with their problems and try to get me involved. Sometimes I feel like running away.

M: This is the knowledge of your concepts, this is not *your* knowledge. To feel that you are involved in the world is a concept, to feel like running away is a concept.

Q: If a person is very sincere and wants Self-realization more than anything else in the world, is it easier for him if he goes away by himself and thinks of nothing but that?

M: Not at all. It is not that you are going to acquire something externally, the knowledge that you are is already there, only understand that.

This is all the play of concepts. Even to think that I am going to get the knowledge, or I have got the knowledge, is still a concept. Prior to getting the knowledge, whatever Is, That is the truth.

Q: When someone asks Maharaj a very difficult question, where does the answer come from?

M: Out of the question the answer comes; with every question the replies are attached.

May 9, 1981

Questioner: If there is a painful illness, does the jnani *suffer it like anyone else?*

Maharaj: In the case of a *jnani* the mind and intellect do not function. They do not register what is being suffered, but the suffering is even more intense because in the case of an individual it is the body which suffers. In the case of a *jnani* it is the consciousness that suffers, so anything that is experienced in consciousness becomes exaggerated many times more. But you need not bother with this stage, because it is a rare case. In the case of a *jnani* the state is that of total disassociation from the body-mind.

As an entity, a certain amount of disassociation with the body is a pleasing state — a state to which people look forward and accept. In the case of a *jnani,* the disassociation is further and total, therefore there is no question of any effect of such a state, pleasing or otherwise. The result is that there are no wants or desires. This is the way in which I experience — I don't know about others.

Q: Can Maharaj give me knowledge?

M: Understand this: a *jnani* cannot give knowledge to anyone. All he can do is point to that which is your true nature. With such a condition offered here, I don't know why people are attracted to this place. There is nothing I can give anybody who comes here. The attraction to this place is spontaneous and not understandable intellectually.

If what I have been saying is clearly understood by anyone the effective result will be that even in the daily working of the individual's life there will not be any specific intention. Things will continue in a sort of ballbearing fashion — without any deliberate intention or deliberate action. In my own case, throughout the day the body carries out its normal functions; things go on in a normal way and nothing is resisted. Throughout the whole day there is no interest in understanding what is happening.

Up until eight o'clock the intellect did not function; now I am aware of a little perception of my intellect.

In the life of a *jnani,* no *jnani* will expose this secret. Not only will he have no desires or expectations, but neither will he have the attraction "to be." The attraction of the consciousness to be is not there. To have any hopes, expectations, etc., one must have an image, an identity.

May 10, 1981

Maharaj: That which you like most — that itself is "I Am," the conscious presence — but that is not going to last forever.

When this flame is extinguished, what is the profit or loss to the flame? What does the flame represent?

Questioner: The knowledge, the consciousness.

M: What is going to happen to that consciousness? Only in order to realize it, to understand it, do we have all this spirituality. When the flame is extinguished it needs do nothing about itself. Similarly, understand, when the body drops off and the consciousness is extinguished. you need do nothing. With this understanding, do what you like in the world.

Presently you are tied down to the bondage of the body, and that is conceptual. The very thought of any advantage or disadvantage is dissolved when one realizes this knowledge.

For the sake of that principle you are involving yourself in many activities. When that very principle is dissolved into nothingness, what are you going to do?

Don't try to pick and choose, and say "this I must do and that I must not do." Don't impose such conditions on yourself.

An ant crawls on your body and stings you; by that bite or sting you know the ant is there. Just so, the feeling of this conscious presence "I Am" is due to the material body.

Having understood this, where is the person who should hold on to the worldly life or should give it up? The question does not arise.

If you are fully charged with this knowledge, in spite of the worldly difficulties no difficulties will touch you.

This cryptic blunt talk will not be available elsewhere. At other places you will be given certain concepts arising out of consciousness and out of those concepts more concepts are developed, and you are misled. Any type of concept in the realm of consciousness is unreal. Will the world listen to such talks?

What are you? Are you that birth principle, that body, which is born of the secretion of the parents?

The one who gets this knowledge is free from worldly or family problems.

June 6, 1981

Maharaj: The material of which the body is constituted is getting weary and weak, and along with it, this knowledge is also getting weak. The sense of presence is still with me because that material of which the body is made still has a little strength. When that little strength goes away, then the consciousness will also disappear, then there will be no sense of presence — but I shall very much be, without the sense of presence.

Each of you is trying to protect yourself. What is it that you are trying to protect? However much you may protect, how long will it last? Go to the root and find out what it is that you are trying to protect and preserve, and how long it will remain.

The only spiritual way of understanding your true nature is to find out the source of this concept "I Am." Before the sense of presence arrived I was in that state in which the concept of time was never there. So, what is born? It is the concept of time and that event which is birth, living, and death together constitute nothing but time, duration.

Once you understand this, everything will be clear; until you understand it, nothing will be clear. Is this not simple and easy?

Questioner: Words are simple, but apprehending what those words mean will be difficult.

M: What is it in the absence of which you would not be able to understand even the words? Go to the root of that source.

In apprehending what I have told you this morning, the intellect is totally impotent. There must be an intuitive apprehension of it.

June 8, 1981

Maharaj: People don't really understand what I say. They partially understand and form their own concepts, but the real Self knowledge is not there.

Suppose there is a seed which is going to produce a great tree. If you cut that seed you must be able to see the tree in the seed.

The tree which I got is that seed which is called the seed of birth, when I broke it open I got the Self knowledge. Other than Self knowledge, what other capital do I have?

I have met so many so-called *jnanis,* but the real one, who has seen the tree in the seed, I have not seen so far.

In the advanced stages what happens to the intellect? To the disappearance of the intellect at old age, there is a witness. How can you describe that witness?

Questioner: *Thoughts and emotions are always arising and distracting me. What shall I do?*

M: You are before any thought can arise. All thoughts, etc., which arise are merely movements in consciousness.

Once consciousness arises, everything arises — the world and all the transactions in the world. Merely witness them. It takes place, there is no individual to witness. Witnessing takes place of the total functioning of the universal consciousness.

Because I totally negate the individual, this will appeal only to one in a million.

Q: *There are so many people who are thoroughly dissatisfied, always searching for something and never satisfied. Why is that?*

M: You will never be satisfied until you find out that you are what you are seeking. If you want knowledge as an individual, you will not get it here. If you are satisfied with this knowledge, you may come and sit still. If you cannot accept this negating of yourself, you may leave. I will understand, it will not affect me.

That which has never happened at all, that is the child of a barren woman — what fear can you have for that? It is imagined, unreal. Out of that hallucination, if somebody wants something, is it not seeking the real in the totally unreal?

Q: *If it were real then we could do something about it.*

M: Correct. You see something, that is true, but what you see is an illusion, like a dream. What we see in a dream seems very real, but we know that it is unreal.

In spite of understanding all this, still it is difficult to give up this form identity of a male or a female.

Without the form, the knowledge cannot be given. For the Absolute to manifest Itself, the matter must be there. The Absolute unmanifested and the manifested are not two — it is merely the expression of It, like the shadow and the substance.

This love of being is not of an individual being, it is the nature of the entire universal consciousness.

June 11, 1981 (Morning)

Maharaj: It is only when the identity with the body-mind has been firmly rejected and identity with the consciousness has been thoroughly established that what I say will have any meaning.

What you are is the unlimited, which is not susceptible to the senses. By limiting yourself to the body you have closed yourself to the unlimited potential which you really are.

In meditation it is consciousness which meditates on itself and remains within itself.

If you accept what I have told you, then you do not take delivery of what is happening spontaneously in the world, and you are not concerned with either the cause or the effect. You then accept your true nature. Whatever actions take place through the body will take place independently of that which you really are.

Bear in mind that when this life force (that which is the breath and consciousness) leaves the body, it will not seek permission from anything. It came spontaneously and will leave spontaneously; that is all that happens in that which is called death. There is no one who is born or who will die.

Questioner: As I understand it, the purpose of life is merely to understand that what has been manifested and what is functioning is the universal consciousness. Other than understanding, there is nothing to be done. Is this correct?

M: Correct. Everything is spontaneous, automatic, natural, it is only the concept of me and mine that is the bondage.

When simple people like you are here, I am at peace, not disturbed, but when people come who consider themselves *jnanis,* who have the pride of knowledge and wish to show off their knowledge, then there is disturbance.

Q: This is a very high kind of knowledge, at a very high level; until it is absorbed what should an ordinary man do?

M: So long as there is receptivity, a deep desire to understand it, there is nothing to be done. The knowledge itself will result in whatever is to result. It is not mental or intellectual caliber that is required, but an intuitive sense of discrimination.

So, now you are not the body, having accepted it, can you continue to identify with the body?

Q: Do body and mind have an importance?

M: Everything has its importance.

Q: Must we not take care of the body?

M: One takes care of something with which one identifies, but you have nothing to do with body-mind anymore, so why are you concerned in taking care of them?

When you are the space you are no more the body, but whatever is contained in the space, and the space, you are. You are now manifest — whatever is known — the space. This space is known by *chidakash.* When you are the *chidakash* you are subtler than the physical space, expansiveness is more. A *jnani* transcends in various stages these subtleties, skies, spaces. In *chidakash* he is still confined, still conditioned by thinking "I Am," therefore the next is *Paramakash. Paramakash* is the highest, in which there are other *akashes* — seven. In *chidakash* this knowingness is "I Am." In *Paramakash* there is no is or is not, It transcends everything.

June 11, 1981 (Evening)

Questioner: What is love? Does it fulfill a need or pleasure?

Maharaj: Yes. When you see something and you like it, this liking is love for that object. When anger and frustration arise, that too is part of love. It is quite good and very bad also. All the experiences of suffering are the result of love. Find out what is the requisite for all this play of love and hate. It is that love for beingness, existence, which gives rise to all pain and miseries. You have to face it because you love to be. Prior to any love, that love for being is there. It tastes both the qualities of love and misery, pleasure and pain. Take the case of this flame (of the cigarette lighter) it gives the light, the warmth, and it can also burn.

Q: Can I be away from it?

M: What are you that wants to be away from it? If you are apart from me I can keep you out of me, but whatever is is not apart from me.

What is the "you" that has sprouted, that has taken root? That alone is the cause of pleasure and pain.

When you understand this, it is all over — finished. Then you do some clapping, shout and scream out of exuberance; all the show is over. The knowledge I am giving is going to dispel all the so-called knowledge you have.

A *jnani* is subtle like the space. What is the space like? You assume there is the sky — what is it like? This knowledge is subtler than the space. The father of the space is the knowledge "I Am."

Q: How do you know consciousness?

M: The way you started knowing yourself — exactly the same way. When you know that you are it will be the same as acquiring yourself — nevertheless, you were all along, were you not? What is the use of concluding logically? You must say right here and now — here he is — in actuality.

Q: Why does Maharaj take such an interest in me then?

M: Who is taking an interest in whom? Who is having the doership of that? It is all happening spontaneously.

June 13, 1981

Maharaj: In common spiritual parlance knowledge means repeating what you have heard — presentation of intelligence. They think it is spiritual, but no one tries to find out what he is, does not look at himself. When a boy and girl get married they are intensely interested in each other, similarly, when one gets married to spirituality one is always occupied with thoughts or deliberations concerning spirituality.

Are you the blood flowing inside, are you the skin, the bones? You are not. When you investigate thus and come to understand that you are not the body, you will eliminate everything — whatever you are not. Finally, what will you be? Come to this point.

You are so much addicted to the things which you learn by heart, the rituals, the *bhajans,* etc., that unless you recite them every day you will not get any satisfaction of feeling happy.

These ritualistic practices are given for the ignorant, to keep their body-mind busy, but having the body-mind is to know that you are and it has no name or form.

These is no question of pleasure or pain, nor fear of death, for one who understands. If one identifies with the body then one is caught up in the relations related to the body.

My words are few and short, but they are very effective. There are many volumes written about spirituality which do not destroy your concepts, but add to them. All the volumes do not tell you what you are.

Questioner: *What is meant by* chinmayananda *and* sat-chit-ananda?

M: People sometimes dance when they sing *bhajans,* they lose themselves, so that state is called *chinmayananda.* To have that *chinmayananda,* the first touch of consciousness is necessary. *Ananda* means bliss, and this is a quality of mind — a higher realm of the mind — but present in the consciousness. The prerequisite is the kiss of consciousness which is necessary for that highest state of exultation or exhilaration, that is *chinmayananda* and *sat-chit-ananda.*

I have come to the firm conclusion that I am nothing, I have no design, no color, I have no image of myself.

In the early morning when the waking state happens, that kiss of beingness appears, vibrant in the entire universe, and vibrating in myself. Also I observe this same thing when I take rest in the afternoon. But if you want to judge me at a physical level, I am not able to lift this pot of water, that is how much strength is left in the body, but that touch of all the vibrant universe — that is the touch of my "I Amness."

I am the knower of the Brahman, I am the Brahman *jnani,* nevertheless, this touch of beingness is misery only.

June 15, 1981

Maharaj: Once the knowledge has dawned in you, you are a *jnani,* you are no more a human person. You are the manifest Brahman, Chetana, the dynamic manifest Brahman.

Earlier your thoughts used to be connected with the body and the relatives of the body, but having gotten disassociated from the body-mind and established in the state of dynamic consciousness, what could be the quality of your thoughts? Your thoughts will be more subtle, if there are any thoughts. Nevertheless, this dynamic consciousness is the quality of the food body. So long as the body is, the consciousness is.

Whatever you talk and receive in the morning, you will continue repeating until you fall into sleep; nobody inquires at this level — all this functioning — how does it happen? What is the quality of this functioning and how does it occur? What are you? Inquire into it.

Only a few people are capable of understanding this. That is why I send people away — because it is of no use, just listening to words — but if that firm faith is there what I say will dawn in them. The inadequacies of the intellect should be made up by this very strong faith.

Beingness is there, the consciousness is there, and because it is there, the world is there. When the consciousness only prevails, when people talk, I don't understand; only the conscious presence is felt and not the details of what is happening. Because of the conscious presence you count me as present; if the consciousness is not there, you will say I am not present.

June 17, 1981

[The questioner was quoting scriptures right and left.]

Maharaj: The moment the waking state starts the worshipping of misery begins. When did you have the first birth?

Questioner: *I don't know anything about it.*

M: Then how do you accept this about the Ultimate? This is not your direct experience, it is borrowed knowledge from books. How can you accept what is not your direct experience?

There was a robbery in Delhi, the police may arrest you here and accuse you of it. Have you ever been to Delhi?

Q: *No.*

M: Then why did you accept this birth? What are *shastras* or scriptures? It is merely the do's and don'ts on how we should behave in the world. Don't bring that here. Whether you accept this birth or not was the original question. Why bring in all this tall talk? Reading scriptures is all right for the ignorant. The next step is to give it up and try to understand what you are.

Shake off all that you have read and try to understand now. You must apply your discrimination. It is of no use just blindly accepting what the scriptures have said. Accept them up to a certain stage — after that you must be strong enough or mature enough to use your discrimination. People move about in search of knowledge but they are caught up in the trap of words and in the fond concepts developed by so-called Sages. A certain Sage will ask you to behave in one way; you go to another Sage and he will have you behave in another way. Thus you are caught up in the concepts of others. There is the story of a *rishi* in the scriptures who drank the waters of the seven oceans in one handful — are you going to believe this? Employ your discrimination. You speak of *acharana,* the code of behavior; *charana* means the one who has to behave. *charana* means only "I love" state, "I Am" state, the state of consciousness, the feeling of being, without words. From that condition the movement in consciousness begins.

Loki and aloki: loki we normally take as worldly; *lok* means various personalities. Whatever is prescribed by the personality is *loki,* or whatever is followed by the people. *Aloki* is transcending the worldly. *Aloki,* it is not known to you. These devotees love me, but they don't understand me in the *aloki* sphere.

Spiritual talk is *lokic* talk, common talk, trying to give an image to others. Here there is no image or design — now, how can you become one with that? You have to have an image or design. Whatever knowledge we talk about has to be communicated by words, but that is not the Ultimate.

You want to possess knowledge, to collect knowledge. Such knowledge is plentiful and available in the world, but a rare person will understand that such knowledge is a bundle of ignorance.

You will make a study of those concepts which erupt from you; those concepts which you do not like will not occur to you. If you are interested in spiritual living, your thoughts and concepts will relate to that.

I have said what I have to say. There is no question of saying anything more. Because you come here I treat you with courtesy, but I am fully convinced that you and I have no design. I am afraid that what I say will not reach your real core; therefore you do *bhajans.* As a matter of fact, you should not visit me at all.

Bhishwa was on a bed of arrows in his last days; I am also on a bed of arrows of suffering.

June 26, 1981

Maharaj: For those who are sitting here the benefit you get will not be different from the benefit you get sitting under the shade of several thickly leaved trees. Sitting under the trees there is a certain amount of peace and the feelings of well-being. Stay in peace.

My teachings are emanating out of this consciousness. It is like a big shady tree for relaxation; you come here and sit and feel the relaxation, but you are not able to say what it is like. In that state you are not able to explain by words. You are in a relaxed state but the deeper meaning is reveling in the Self, abiding and subsiding in the Self — that is why you feel relaxed and happy.

Whatever sentences you hear in this state will not be forgotten.

Swartha — *swa* means Self and *artha* — meaning. *Swartha* has great meaning. *Swartha* means selfishness and *swa* means the meaning of the Self. Words have meaning in the practical world which will make you selfish, but the words which emanate here will give you the meaning of your own Self.

[A mother and son came and garlanded Maharaj and distributed prasad *to everyone present.]*

M: The deep state of simple, innocent people comes to fruition in this fashion. She prayed that her son would pass the examination. Her own faith worked.

If you enjoy this relaxed state here, and if you become one with this state, you will also transcend this state. You will even transcend into a state prior to the birth of Gods.

With this understanding, do what you like. Carry out your worldly activities. When you understand the meaning of *swa* — the Self — there will be no room for selfishness.

Understand this thoroughly, abide in it, then in due course you will realize it. When the time is ripe, only then it will happen.

What is your worth? You are the consciousness through which the world is expressed. Abide in that worthiness. Don't step down into mind and the body. Again, you must have the firm conviction that you are unaffected by birth and death. You are like space, not only like space, you are prior to space.

That Ultimate *you* can never be lost. Whatever you have lost, you have lost only the words.

I have told you enough and whatever you have heard, retain it, deliberate over it, ponder over it, and be one with that.

July 1, 1981

Questioner: Deep sleep is no-knowing. The Absolute is beyond knowingness and no-knowingness. I do not understand.

Maharaj: To start with, a child is born: the infant does not know itself, the reactions of hunger, thirst, etc., take place. These are physical things, when life is there, but inside that state knowingness has not developed or matured fully. After one or two years it comes to know itself, the mother, etc. When the child knows itself, its knowingness has started.

Prior to that it is ignorance, although it is no-knowingness, it is ignorance. Then the knowledge "I Am" is attained: it does not know *who* it is but it knows it is *something.* Later on the child starts collecting concepts and ideas which other people feed it and develops certain concepts or images about itself and others. The mind has developed. Then comes deep sleep and the waking state, the daily cycle. In the waking state, in whatever state of mind you are, you know the world, together with your concepts and then you fall into sleep. Now, technically, you can call that deep sleep no-knowingness. But this is not that no-knowingness beyond which the Absolute lies.

Let us proceed again from the child. Ignorance, knowingness, accumulation of concepts, meeting the Guru. The Guru tells you, "Get rid of concepts, just be yourself." So, when you are, only *you* are. This is the first step: to abide in the consciousness that you are, without words — that is knowledge. When the child started knowing itself there was also knowledge — but that is a general knowledge and is common to all. This becomes spiritual now. The seeker, having understood what the Guru said, gets rid of the concepts, and now, as the first step, the seeker dwells in the state "I Am," just being.

First of all there is the knowingness "I Am," without words; with that knowingness the world is. Now when the seeker goes into meditation, that knowingness goes into no-knowingness. This is the highest in the hierarchy when the body aspect is there because this knowing and no-knowing are aspects of the body, and body means consciousness, and in the realm of consciousness knowingness and no-knowingness exist.

The Absolute transcends knowingness and no-knowingness. So, no-knowingness is the highest in the hierarchy of spirituality, and the destination is transcendence of knowingness and no-knowingness.

Q: I thought no-knowingness means the Absolute.

M: Knowingness and no-knowingness are the expressions of the bodily consciousness. When this food instrument body, together with the consciousness is totally transcended — that is the Absolute.

The light is there, the darkness is there, but what is the background? The space. The space is there which is neither the light nor the dark, but the space *is.* You have to transcend light and darkness to abide in space. Similarly, one has to transcend the knowingness and no-knowingness — the aspects of bodily consciousness. If you have reached that state you are watching consciousness and no-consciousness. That is called natural *samadhi,* or *sahaja samadhi.*

Naturally you are in that state, but this psychosomatic instrument of body and consciousness is always available. The moment somebody comes the instrument is being operated — otherwise you revert to the Absolute. It is something like this: in a big hall there is a door, and in the door is a peep hole. That peep hole is the consciousness, but you are at the back.

Suppose that those space ships are going up from the earth: when you are in the space you feel that you have escaped the earth, but it is not so — you are still under the influence of the earthly atmosphere. You must go further into the space where there is no atmosphere. But where is the thought of your going there? It is not like that — you are truly the Absolute and these are all the coverings you have gotten.

You know you are but you forget that you are and that forgetfulness is no-knowingness, which is the highest state. You can never describe it by words; that state is never captured by words.

Understanding is necessary and you should not get confused. Suppose you live in a state of knowingness: you should not think that you are a *jnani* already simply because your knowingness receives many powers in that state. You might think you are a *jnani,* but it is not so — it is simply the first step. There are a lot of allurements at that stage. When you are only being, without words, you are powerful. Give up the powers, don't possess them.

Glossary

Advaita: Non-dualism. The doctrine which contends that only the Absolute — the ultimate principle, has existence, and that all phenomenal existence is illusion.

Adya: Primordial; original.

Agni: Fire.

Aham: I; the ego.

Ajnana: Ignorance.

Akasha: Ether; the sky.

Ananda: Bliss; happiness; joy.

Arati: Divine service performed in the early morning or at dusk.

Asana: Posture; seat.

Ashram: Hermitage.

Atma, Atman: The Self.

Avatar: Divine incarnation.

Bhagavan: The Lord.

Bhajan: Devotional practice; worship.

Bhakta: Devotee.

Bhakti: Devotion; love.

Bija: Seed; source.

Brahman: God as creator.

Brahma-randhra: Opening in the crown of the head; fontanelle.

Buddhi: Intellect.

Chaitanya: Consciousness.

Chakra: Plexus.

Chidakasha: Mental ether (all-pervading).

Chit: Universal consciousness.

Chitta: Mind stuff.

Darshan: Viewing; seeing.

Deva: Divine being.

Dharma: Code of conduct.

Ganapati: A Hindu deity; success-bestowing aspect of God.

Gayatri: Sacred Vedic mantra.

Gita: Song.

Guna: Quality born of nature; attribute.

Guru: Teacher; preceptor.

Hanuman: A powerful deity; the son of the Wind God; a great devotee of Sri Rama; the famous monkey who helped Rama in his fight with Ravana.

Hiranyagarbha: Cosmic intelligence; cosmic mind; cosmic egg.

Iswara: God.

Japa: Repetition of God's name; repetition of a mantra.

Jiva: The individual soul.

Jnana: Knowledge.

Jnani: The knower.

Kalpana: Imagination of the mind.

Kama: Desire; lust.

Karma: Action.

Karta: Doer.

Kendra: Center; heart.

Kosa: Sheath.

Kriya: Physical action.

Kumbhaka: Retention of breath.

Kundalini: The primordial cosmic energy located in the individual.

Laya: Dissolution; merging.

Lila: Play, sport.

Linga: Symbol.

Maha: Great.

Mahasamadhi: The death of a spiritual preceptor.

Mahattava: The great principle.

Mana: Mind; the thinking faculty.

Manana: Constant thinking; reflection; meditation.

Manolaya: Involution and dissolution of the mind into its cause.

Mantra: Sacred syllable or word or set of words.

Marga: Path or road.

Mauna or Mouna: Silence.

Maya: The illusive power of Brahman; the veiling and projection of the universe.

Mumukshu: Seeker after liberation.

Muni: A sage; an austere person.

Nama: Name.

Namarupa: Name and form; the nature of the world.

Neti-Neti: "Not this, not this"; negating all names and forms in order to arrive at the underlying truth.

Nirguna: Without attributes.

Nisarga: Nature; the natural state.

Pandit: A learned man; a scholar.

Para: Supreme.

Parabrahman: The Supreme; the Absolute.

Paramatman: The Supreme Self.

Prajna: Higher consciousness; awareness.

Prakriti: Causal matter; cosmic substance.

Prana: Vital energy; life breath.

Prema: Divine love.

Puja: Worship.

Purna: Full; complete; infinite.

Purusha or Purusa: The Self which abides in the heart of all things; the cosmic spirit.

Rajas: One of the three aspects of cosmic energy; passion; restlessness; activity. One of the *gunas.*

Sadhaka: Spiritual aspirant.

Sadhana: Spiritual practice.

Sagunabrahman: The Absolute conceived of as endowed with qualities.

Sakti or Shakti: Power; energy; force.

Samadhi: Oneness; here the mind becomes identified with the object of meditation.

Samsara: The process of worldly life.

Samskara: Impression.

Sankalpa: Thought; desire; imagination.

Sat: Existence; being.

Sat-Chit-Ananda: Existence-knowledge-bliss.

Satsang: Association with the wise.

Satva or Sattwa: Light; purity.

Siddha: A perfected Yogi.

Siddhi: Psychic power.

Swarupa: Essence; essential nature; one's own form.

Tamas: Darkness; inertia; one of the *gunas.*

Upanishad: Knowledge portion of the Vedas.

Vac or Vak: Speech.

Vasana: Subtle desire.

Vayu: The Wind God; air; vital breath.

Veda: A scripture of the Hindus.

Vedanta: The end of the Vedas.

Vichara: Inquiry into the nature of the Self.

Vijnana: Principle of pure intelligence.

Vritti: Thought-wave; mental modification.

Yoga: Union; the philosophy of the sage Paranjali teaching the union of the individual with God.

Yogi: One who is an adept in Yoga.